GET LIT
STAY LIT
SPREAD IT

KELLY K

GET LIT
STAY LIT
SPREAD IT

Igniting a fire for God that never burns out

Published by Kelly K Ministries
1900 S 13th St | Kingfisher, Oklahoma 73750 USA

Front cover design by Ian Lundin
www.CXXIIapparel.com
Book design copyright © 2020 Kelly K Ministries. All rights reserved.
Published in the United States of America

www.KellyKMinistries.com
ISBN-13: 9798610423319

ENDORSEMENTS

"Kelly K is definitely a man after Gods own heart, with a passion to see people build a personal relationship with Jesus. I remember bringing my sons to a youth event that Kelly was apart of. I let them listen to the message from Kelly, who happened to be the main speaker that night. "Get Lit, Stay Lit, Spread It" was the message. Weeks went by and I was surprised to hear my 8-year-old bring that message up at dinner, explaining what we are to do as followers of Christ! Kelly broke it down in such a way that my son was able to relate to the lingo, and actually explain to me what "stay lit" and "spread it" was all about. It made me proud as a father to hear my son break down the beginnings of The Great Commission in his own way. I'm excited see the impact this book will have on this generation and generations to come.

Get Lit Baby!"

- Shonlock
Christian Hip Hop Artist

"I've known Kelly K for a long time. Since the early days of our band, RED. He is a man of passion and a true follower of God. His new book will challenge

you and encourage you to never give up and keep fighting. The struggle is real, but in our suffering, God can make us whole. Be sure to give my good friend Kelly K's book a read! You won't regret it."

- Michael Barnes
"RED"

"I had the good fortune to work with Kelly last year on tour with my band Wang Chung. He quickly became a key member of the Wang Chung family and in the process I got to know him and his work and mission outside of what he was doing for us. It fascinated me and we had numerous stimulating conversations about God, Jesus, life, spirituality and the Universe, as well as Kelly's own life stories. Apart from Kelly's abundance of life experience both good and bad, his down to earth honesty, integrity, intelligent insight, and of course faith, I found fascinating and stimulating. I even read his first book, which had exactly the same effect on me. I enjoy his ability to deal with so many universal elements but at the same time to humanize them and express them in

ways that we all can understand. Much like Jesus was able to do. I have also since checked out some of his preaching appearances online and found them very effective and helpful.

So I recommend Kelly the man, the preacher and his writings.

Apart from that he's pretty terrible and he doesn't buy me enough croissants."

- **Nick Feldman**
"Wang Chung"

"Kelly K is a true evangelist at heart. He is a fire-breathing, devil-stoping, soul-winning, WILD kind of Christ-follower. His passion for Jesus is contagious and his obvious love for people is inspiring. This modern-day John the baptist is a fire-brand! Enjoy his newest book!"

- **Kemtal Glasgow**
Multi-generational speaker & Associate Pastor Gateway Church

"I have had the privilege of knowing Kelly for the last 3.5 years. We travelled together in close quarters on a youth tour, and I can tell you one thing for certain, he lives what he preaches.

From the early days of doing random acts of kindness for people in Walmart's all over America to preaching for free hundreds of times. Not because he had the money or because he had nothing better to do; but because the message that he writes about in this book he lives out every single day.

Kelly isn't a fair weather Christ follower. He is one of the most passionate men I've ever met about anything. We have sat at numerous Buffalo Wild Wings restaurants all across America, and I've heard story after story of how the consuming fire of Heaven has infiltrated every part of him. That fire in him is contagious and something that he has an authority to speak and write about.

I remember the first time I heard him speak the message "Get Lit," telling funny stories of his life and compelling people that this fire is one that is for all. It wasn't just a message he spoke, but words I myself had actually watch him live.

This book is perfect if you need a stirring of your faith, you want a fresh fire, or if you want to continue living fired up to make a mark on the world you live in.

It will truly will help you "get lit, stay lit, and spread it."

I pray as you read this, it pushes you to live bigger than you are right now. I pray that the words that Kelly has labored over will inspire you for more of Jesus and to pass Jesus on to all those around you!
Reaching and Impacting the World BY ANY MEANS NECESSARY."

- Joel Bennett
Pastor & Evangelist
BAMN International

Acknowledgments

Lindsay, Brennen, Chase, Avery, and Jaxx - Thank you for allowing me to travel all over the world and set fires! Thank you for loving me through all my crazy ideas and plans. Thank you for always going to movies with me that I know none of you want to see. Thank you for laughing at my dad jokes. Thank you for not leaving me during my "long hair" phase. Thank you for allowing me to be a part of the most incredible family in the world. I absolutely adore you all, and I love you more than you will ever know!

Harlan and Susan Robertson - Thank you so much for believing in me, praying for me, loving me, and supporting me. You took the time to get to know me when you didn't have to at all, and we built an amazing relationship over the one common thing between us. Jesus. Without your support, this book would have never been possible. I am so absolutely grateful for the two of you, and I will never stop thanking God for putting you both in my life at just the right time!

Norma Jean Lutz - I am so grateful for your smiling face and powerful prayers every time I'm with you. Thank you for your help on this book. Your wisdom, insight, and hard work is greatly appreciated. Thank you!

Ian Lundin - Thank you so much for designing the perfect cover for this book! You have a way of making the vision in my heard turn out even better than I dreamed. Thank you for all the work you've done for me, the amazing clothes you hook me up with, and most importantly, thank you for being an awesome friend!

Jarrod Kopp - Thank you for pointing out that you were the ONLY family member I DIDN'T thank in my last book. Look at you now! You're welcome!

TABLE OF CONTENTS

SECTION THREE: Spread it

SECTION ONE - GET LIT

_____ *Chapter One* _____

THE GREAT TULSA DUMPSTER FIRE

Okay, I'm just going to tell it like it is right from the beginning. I know you think you have an awesome grandma, but there is no question in my mind that the Lord God himself chose two of the greatest grandmothers in the world to bless me with. No contest. First, if you recall from my first book, Reckless Love Revolution, my dad's mom, Mema, made the world's best cookies, which for a confirmed chubby kid was like having a leprechaun bringing me gold on a daily basis. However, it was my mom Echo's mother, Mimi, who really knew the way to my heart.

She was like the cool grandma in an 80s movie. You know, the one that chain smokes, and lets the grandkids do whatever, because you're only a kid once. Her apartment, near the Arkansas River in Tulsa, Oklahoma, was one of my favorite places to be. However, one stay there when I was nine or ten years old stands out as one of the highlights of my childhood.

I'd been dying to see Rambo First Blood. I hadn't asked, because I knew what my parents' answer would be, and if I'd put it on her radar, my mom would have put a stop to it before I even asked Mimi. So, when we rolled up to the Blockbuster store, and Mimi offered to let me choose, I didn't even hesitate. It was everything my violent young heart had hoped, and more. But it paled in comparison to what happened next.

If you're too young to know what Rambo is, I'm sorry your childhood wasn't as epic as mine. To be real though, he was a good example of what happens when violence is your go-to solution. It rarely ends well. As for Blockbuster—it may surprise you to learn that Netflix hasn't always existed. There used to be businesses in every town in America that rented DVDs. Yes, those things you can buy for a $1 at Walmart rented for as much as $5 a night!

On a high from my violence-filled fantasies, I decided to head down to one of my favorite spots along the banks of the Arkansas river. I don't remember why I was there because I found something that changed my life. There, left behind by some careless teen no doubt, was one of the most beautiful things I'd seen in my young life. There, lying on the red clay was a bright red plastic rectangle that made my heart jump into my throat. I'd seen these a lot. It was a Bic lighter.

I'd been sneaking my grandma's lighter and cigarettes from time to time for a while, and my mind went crazy with the possibilities that me and this lighter could get up to. I was a big fan of fire and here in the palm of my hand was the key to unlocking my bliss. Now, I just needed something to burn.

As I headed back to the apartment, lighter in hand, a thought crossed my mind. Even Mimi might not be cool enough to let a 10-year-old kid have his own lighter. So, I tucked it safely in my pocket and headed in to plan my blaze. I needed something that would burn easily without causing any real damage, and I was sure I could find something. What happened was like the clouds parting and an angel from heaven handing me my dreams on a golden platter.

"Kelly," Mimi called. "I've got all of these wire hangers from the dry cleaner's and I don't need them. Would you take this bunch of hangers out to the dumpster for me?"

It couldn't be this easy, could it? As I eyed the paper triangles in each of those beautiful wire hangers, the lighter burned a metaphorical hole in my jeans pocket. They were perfect. They'd burn easily, they were already going to the trash, no one would miss them, and I'd get to watch them burn. It was like a dream. At this point, I'll share a bit of wisdom. When things in life just fall into place perfectly, one of two things may be happening.

One, God could be opening a door for you. It does happen. Two, God could be presenting you with a test to see if you'll make a good choice. In my experience, this is more often the case. At that moment in time, though, God was the last thing on my mind. All I saw was flames dancing in my imagination. Besides, who was I hurting? I hadn't stolen the lighter or the hangers, so it was a win-win.

"Sure, Mimi," I said, trying to play it cool. I didn't want her catching on to what I was about to do. "I'll be glad to take those to the dumpster for you."

"You're a sweet boy, Kelly."

As I walked towards that dumpster, I know I must have looked ridiculous, but I felt like John J Rambo swaggering into combat against the evil sheriff. I held the lighter in my palm, the stack of hangers under my arm as I turned the corner and saw that beautiful metal dumpster. It was perfect.

I walked up, checking my surroundings. In my experience, a kid doing anything suspicious would get called down by any conscious adult, and I couldn't risk getting caught. The coast was clear as I thumbed the flame to life and held the first hanger over that brilliant orange and blue tongue.

It licked greedily, darkening the paper until it burst into life, I threw it quickly into the dumpster and lit the rest. I felt on top of the world. My heart thudded in my chest.

As I turned and started back to Mimi's apartment, my joy turned to terror with a whoosh. As I looked back, to my horror, I watched as the entire contents of the dumpster caught on fire, the flames dancing in the pupils of my widening eyes, the lighter like a lead weight in my hand as the flames crawled up, out of the dumpster, higher and higher, chewing greedily at the wall of the nearest apartment building, much closer than I'd realized.

My feet were frozen to the ground, even as a part of my brain was screaming RUN! That's when I learned something so important, it's stuck with me to this day and it's a big part of the reason for this book. People show up when there's a fire.

First, it was just one.

"Oh, dang!"

Then another.

"Somebody, call the fire department!"

People shouted and ran, more and more of them were coming out to see the fire I'd started and I just knew they knew it was me. Since this was before everyone had a cell phone, someone had run inside to call and was now back.

"The fire department is on their way!"

"Well, I hope they show up faster than the last time, it's really burning quick!"

The second part of my realization was this. There are two kinds of people who show up to a fire. The first are those who want to watch it burn. Whether they stand in amazement or perhaps in terror, they are just there to watch it burn.

But soon enough, another type of people will show up, those who want to put the fire out. Make no mistake, someone will always get the idea of putting it out. About three minutes into my own personal horror movie, the Tulsa Fire Department showed up, quickly getting the blaze under control, and almost as fast as it had started, it was out.

"Did you see what happened?" an officer asked. He was looking at me.

"No, it wasn't on fire, and then it was. I don't know. Sun's pretty bright today, maybe somebody threw a magnifying glass in there."

Now, if you're a parent like I am now, you know. You know that those TPD officers took one look at me, sneaking that red Bic into my jeans pocket and they knew. I'm sure there was a hushed conference with the commanding officer on the scene. I'd guess it went something like this.

"That kid did it."

"Yeah, magnifying glass. Did he think we'd believe that?"

"He looks pretty shook up."

Sigh. "No need to wreck a ten-year-old's life, nobody was hurt, a sheet of siding and everything's okay."

"You think he's okay, Sarge?"

"Kid looks terrified, I doubt he'll try this again."

The truck rolled away, leaving a steaming charred mark and a dumpster full of blackened, discarded furniture, and one little boy who was not nearly as scared as they'd thought. I decided right then that I would do this again, more carefully of course, but it was way too awesome to leave alone.

Why, Kelly? Why are you sharing stories of your delinquent past with impressionable young minds? Okay, this is the only PSA you're going to get on this, so pay attention.

Fire is not a toy. It destroys lives. It can kill. It isn't funny. There are plenty of safe ways to experiment with fire and if you're too young to do it on your own, talk to your parents about safe, controlled ways, like campfires, weenie roasts, candles, fireplaces, but do not under any circumstances assume that paper hangers will not burn the world down, because they will.

What I learned about fire from this and other events that will remain untold due to "statutes of limitations" not being up yet, didn't really come into focus until much later. In the next chapter, so that you get the whole picture, I'm going to take you up to what they call the thousand-yard view, and we'll go way back to the beginning.

So lock yourself in and get ready to take a ride with me! The first section of this book is going to lay a foundation of what the fire of God really is, and what His fire is all about. Then we will take it a step further and look at how to get lit ourselves and actually STAY lit instead of being just another "burnt out" Christian. Lastly, we will finish with a full understanding of how to not only stay on fire ourselves, but actually spread that fire to others, and fulfill the Great Commission that Jesus has called us ALL to be apart of. Which ultimately gives us the fulfillment in life that we've always been searching for!

This journey we're about to take together has completely changed my life. If you will open your heart and mind to receive a fresh revelation from Jesus, I know the same is about to happen for you!

Chapter Two

LET THERE BE LIGHT

When the universe was new, God existed. And we don't know what inspired God's desire for a creation, but we know this, God decided to do a little craft project, and part of that was Earth. The Bible says it like this.

In the beginning, God Created the Heavens and the Earth.

You've heard this before, but have you really thought about it? The entire universe coming out of a single intelligence is probably the most staggering fact of life there is. Everything we see, taste, touch, hear, and experience, and everything there is to be experienced in a universe that science tells us is still growing, came from one "mind." I put mind in quotes, because I know this much-- the "mind" of God, is nothing like the three pounds of flesh inside my skull.

I'm a pretty creative dude, but writing an entire sermon sometimes wears me out. So I can't even begin to imagine laying out the plans for this place, let alone constructing it. How much brain power does it take to make all of those species fit into a sustainable ecosystem? To know that one of them will be food for another, but shade for someone else.

It's all so intricately connected it boggles my mind. If you don't know what I mean, get a magnifying glass some time and pick a patch of tall grass in the spring or summer. The activity down there is staggering, all of the different bugs, and larvae, and spiders.

Now blow that up to a square mile, then figure there are 196,000,000 square miles on earth, and almost all of it is completely covered in life, even the desert, even the frozen tundra where it seems nothing could survive.

That's cool, but what I want to get to is a little further on, because the Bible says some kind of interesting stuff right up front. It tells us that the world was empty and dark, and there was chaos down here. This makes me wonder what it would be like to be an intergalactic explorer dropping onto some vacant planet with gases swirling and bubbling lava and a lot of darkness and nothingness.

And when I think about this next part, it makes total sense. Anytime I go to work on a project at my house, or in the garage, one of the first things I do when I get ready to build or fix something, is get some light.

So, picture this. God is swirling in, and above and through all of this, because Paul tells us "In Him we live and move and have our being." What exists up until that point, is somehow integrated into the fabric of God, the entire universe is, because we're told there's nowhere that God isn't. I am, is how he described himself. I exist. So, He's got all of the ingredients for this "craft" project He's about to work on and He's spreading it across the cosmos, but before He can get started, He'd like to be able to show it off, so He's going to need illumination. But at this point, it seems, this is a brand-new concept, cosmically speaking. To me this means, God not only invents light, but imagines it first. What must that have been like?

Now, if creating the universe was my gig, I think I would have played this part up a little bit more, I mean, it's the universe's first light show.

The fact that it doesn't say much about it is why I'm convinced this was more of a utilitarian thing. I do find it interesting though, with some of the speeches God is credited with in the Bible, there are some great ones in Job, that he didn't say a whole lot about this creation of light.

Let there be light.

Sometimes I imagine this like a thunder crack, echoing through the vast reaches of nothingness, time and space. Other times, I think God whispered it, with a smile, as he leaned in closer to inspect his project. I think I like that second one better. He's not trying to impress anyone. He's just a craftsman breaking out His tools for another day of what He does.

Then something totally amazing happens. The angels all get together and light the universe's candle. No. Not at all. All it says is this.

And there was light!

He commanded it and it just came into being! And this right here, I believe, is what God has been about since that very moment up until now. We're down here struggling to see what's next, and He's up there encouraging us to just bring more light. Why? Because light brings life and it destroys darkness. In fact, it's the only way to effectively fight the dark. You can curse it all you want; it won't get one bit less dark until you light a candle.

While metaphorically, using light to illuminate God's work is a cool idea, we also know through science that light is one of the things that is necessary for life to flourish. It's essential for so many processes on this planet, like photosynthesis, without which we wouldn't have oxygen or food. Without heat energy from light, we'd still be floating around on a cold dark planet, except not, because we couldn't survive.

One of the things that scientists study is something called a "Goldilocks planet." One that is close enough to a star to have enough light, without being close enough to fry everything with ultraviolet radiation. There are very few in the entire galaxy compared with how many Earth sized planets exist. That power of light is a divine picture of God's relationship to humanity. We need Him to exist.

Another of the most profound things about light is its extraordinary power of revelation. Think about it, if you've ever been scared in a dark room and turned on the light, you know what I mean. Suddenly the black and white world that seemed so scary, is alive with color and shapes that are more familiar as the light reveals the true nature of the world around us. That happens inside the human soul too, on a metaphorical level. As God invades us, we begin to see our true selves. I used to think this was just about exposing the sin and darkness, and that can happen; but it also means shining on the beauty and love, that goodness that is the image of the God in which we were created. That's the kind of message that is worth sharing.

Think about it, as followers of Jesus we're called to continue his work of love and service to all, bringing the light. There's this really cool verse in Matthew 4. Jesus has just come out of the wilderness being personally tested by Satan, and He's about to start his preaching ministry. This is the prequel to maybe the greatest sermon of all time, the Sermon on the Mount.

The Bible tells us that he had been living in Nazareth, which is the hometown most people referred to when speaking of Jesus. But God's plan was so intricate, that he needed a change of address from Nazareth to Capernaum, just to fulfill Isaiah's prophecy that's quoted in Matthew 4. But it's what the prophecy says that I find really cool.

In the ancestral lands of Zebulun and Naphtali, along the way of the sea, past the Jordan River, in Galilee where the Gentiles live. Among the people living in darkness there, a light shines, a great light. Even there, where people live in the land of the shadow of death, dawn is coming.

Whoa. I get chills typing that. The land of the shadow of death is this world, this temporary place where the Bible says rust decays and thieves break in and steal. This place where the only way out is death. Jesus is not saying we're taking our light and we're leaving. No. He's saying He showed up to light the place on fire! Not for destruction, but to plant the Kingdom of Heaven on earth in the hearts of his followers.

Light is a life-giving force. Light is necessary for humans to survive and thrive, and not just us but every species on the planet. Very few of them can survive without sunlight, or the climate control provided by the sun's warming rays. Light, in fact, is so valuable, that in places where the sun's rays can't reach, plant and animal life will develop what is known as "bioluminescence." It's the same stuff lighting bugs use to blink their light. These creatures in the dark places of the earth, literally generate their own light!

Do you get that? God's first "invention" as it were, in creating the earth is so powerful and so useful that creatures who can't get it from our star, the sun, will develop their own sources! Wow. That's a pretty clear indication of God at work in His creation.

What an amazing feat. And that One Mind designed and built all of this, including the fact that our main source of light is a huge billowing, flaming ball of gas that if we moved just a little closer to, we'd be sucked into its gravity and disintegrated into ash on its molten surface without ever even disturbing it.

It encourages me to know that I'm not the first man to ever think about all of this.

In fact, the Bible gives us examples going right back to almost the beginning. David in Psalm 8 talks about how amazing it is, that with all of this work to his credit, God even notices us.

When I stare into heaven and watch the stars, I think about this as the work of your fingers. I track the moon across the sky and the stars all in their places, and I know that you set this in order. So, why me God? What am I? Why are you merciful to men? Why do you care for our sons and daughters?

This simple shepherd, who ended up being king, was thinking about all of this centuries before Galileo invented the first telescope. Thousands of years before the first man dreamed up a way to leave the earth and send himself hurtling out toward the stars. Light has a powerful draw on the human imagination.

The prophet Isaiah said it like this in chapter 40.

Look up, open your eyes to the stars. Who made them? The same one who causes them to shine, each one in its time and place. He has numbered them, and given each one of them a name. It's because God is so huge we can't even imagine his strength, that he's able to keep them all spinning, so that not one is out of order.

We know that this same God who invents light, also calls Himself Light. Jesus described himself by this name several times. One of my favorites is in John 8.

I am not just here to push back darkness, I'm the very light that will push it back, the light of the whole world shines through me. Anyone that chooses to walk my path and follow my teachings won't walk in darkness. Instead, they too will have the light of life shining through them.

But this God of light doesn't show up to blow us out and blind us! He's not here to bring the searchlight into our lives and find us out. It's not like that.

Instead, when He showed up, He became just like us. Not some angelic being; He lived thirty-three years in a human body, and allowed Himself to be affected by the same darkness we all experience—both the physical darkness of night, and the metaphorical darkness of evil.

He sought out those who were trapped in the political darkness of their day: the tax collectors, the prostitutes, and the Samaritans. It was as if by contrast He would show his light in a darkened world to prove that light was not just for a few, but for everyone.

I think the Bible presents an interesting metaphor here between fire and light. When you go out to your garage (like we talked about earlier), to work on your car, or build that science project for school, you just flip a switch. If your garage is set up right, you'll have plenty of light almost instantly. But the world Jesus entered into was nothing like that.

Technology, as we know it today didn't exist. In Jesus time, it would be almost two thousand years before the first electric light bulb. Today we live in a world that is swamped in artificial light. No joke. It's so prevalent that in some places the light actually changes the living patterns of nocturnal animals. It makes common insects like fireflies, balance on the edge of extinction in areas in and around large cities.

In Biblical Galilee, there were no televisions, radios, or laptops. Not even a hairdryer, curling iron, or rechargeable cordless drill. Everything they wanted in life had to be made by hand, and light was no different. In fact, most things were done in the daylight hours, since light after sundown was not only scarce, but an expense that many could not afford.

Jesus talks about this. He uses language that includes phrases like "the light of day." He tells us to work because darkness is coming. In the ancient world, almost everything you did work-wise had to be done between sunup and sundown, because the dark was dangerous.

There were no giant floodlights for highway construction projects to run 24 hours a day. There were no streetlights to help you find your way home. If you wanted light, you had to bring it with you, and even then, it wouldn't be much.

The reason that darkness is still, to this day, almost synonymous with evil is that in the ancient world, it was deadly. The things that were big enough to hunt a man lived for darkness. Our modern way of thinking is imagining the luxury provided by portable electric lighting. Think about it. How often would you go out at night if it meant lighting a fire, or carrying a torch, just to see where you were going?

In fact, at night, even ancient homes were very dim inside. They were built of clay bricks similar to adobe, and any windows they had, were small because when winter came, they had to be insulated. So, the best guess we have today of all the light inside a home in Jesus' time was the same as if you tried to light your living room with a single 40-watt bulb, or a couple of bright flashlights.

Since there was no electricity, what was the source of the light? Follow me here, because I'm about to take you on a tour of some imagery regarding fire and light, and God's presence. I think you'll find this really cool. It blows my mind every time I think about it.

Through archaeological research, we know that homes were lit with lamps that burned oil—typically olive oil—which was plentiful and relatively inexpensive. Ultimately, the needed result was fire! The homes were lit by the tiny flames of fire produced by one or more clay, olive-oil lamps. They looked similar to the one you see in the movies that Aladdin used to bring forth the genie. This is cool, because what I'm about to show you will definitely release the genie in your life when it comes to serving God!

In Psalm 119, David compares the presence of God lighting our way, to a lamp.

God, every word you speak is like a lamp on the path so that my feet won't stumble. I have promised you that I will be an honest, upright and fair judge, following your ideas of justice, and I will do it.

To sum up light in a single passage, I would quote Jesus in Matthew 5

Just as I am the light, you are the light of this dark world. If you build a town on a hill, it would be hard to hide it from travelers, wouldn't it? You are that town, that city, that Kingdom, and it's like your own lamps at home. When you light them, you don't put bowls over them, do you? That would be silly. That's what lampstands are for, like that city on a hill, they lift the lamp up, where the light can spread into every corner of your home so that everyone can see better.

Listen carefully, this is what I want for you. I want you to be like that city, like that lampstand. I want you to burn so bright in front of people that they can see the good things you're doing. When they do, they'll know you belong to God and they'll thank him for sending you.

How much different would you live if you walked every day with Jesus lifting you up, instead of an image of Jesus scolding you for your sin? What if you really believed that you were the light? And not only that, but that God Himself wanted to put you on display for your kindness and love to others? That's what this passage is saying to us.

Through the rest of this book we're going to talk a lot about fire and light. But for the moment, let's pause before going further into understanding of what the Bible says about fire and light. Just sit still and listen—because every one of us needs to hear this. If you are a child of God, this light burns in you. Not your neighbor, your pastor, your mom, your dad or your goody-goody sister. It's you. You are the lamp. You are the one that Jesus wants to set up as a light to the nations. You are the light of the world. That's you.

It's not about how you feel, or even what your life looks like right now. It's not, and it never has been. It's about Him. It's about His choosing you, and you answering Him. It's about the good work He started in you. It's about Paul's statement in Chapter 1 of Philippians. (I think it's safe to say this is how Jesus feels about us too.)

I am grateful to the Creator every time I remember your face. When I pray for you, it always brings so much joy, because you've partnered with me to teach people about the good news of Jesus from the very beginning. Listen, I'm pretty confident when I say this, God began this good thing in you and He's going to finish it, no matter what. Even if it takes until Jesus comes back.

—————— *Chapter Three* ——————

STRANGE FIRE

If God wants to emphasize something, He repeats it. Those important principles come up again and again in the Bible, through various authors and in different times and places. Lamps and light would be included. In fact, the Bible doesn't mention lamps just a few times, it mentions them more than thirty times.

The more I dig into this, the more I understand why the song, "This Little Light of Mine," is such a powerful way to teach the truth of Jesus to children. It sticks in their mind. It's an easy-to-remember illustration of what God is, what He's about in the earth. It brings it all down to one simple thing—and God is all about one simple thing. Some people seem to think that God is complicated, but even under the Old Testament we find things like this from the prophet Micah in Chapter 6.

Is God like us? Would he be impressed if you sacrificed a million rams, or poured out barrels and barrels of anointing oil? Maybe I should give up my first born child to pay for my mistakes? Would that work? My physical offspring to cover the darkness in my soul?

Pay attention, people, God has shown us over and over what is good. What is it that God wants? It's pretty simple. He wants us to act in justice, to be fair with others. He wants us to be kind and show mercy, and he wants us to have some humility in representing Him.

But as soon as I say that, then I'm going to turn around and explain one of the most complicated ways God ever asked us to interact with Him. I think He did this for a reason. Some say the tabernacle and temple worship were partly for Israel. They had been in Egypt, a land filled with complex religious traditions. Had He just shown up and asked them to just walk with Him as he did with Abraham and Noah, they might not have respected it. The symbolism also served to remind them of their history with God. Either way, fire and light played a big role.

I want to issue a warning right now before we move on with this chapter. I'm about to lay a foundation here, that you will need for the rest of this book. If you've ever seen the foundation to home, you know they aren't pretty. There is nothing thrilling about them. But they play a vital role in keeping that house solid and firm. This will not be the most exciting chapter you read, but trust me when I tell you, what read here is solid and will be a common thread throughout the rest of our journey together.

In the plans God gave Moses to build the tabernacle, He gave instructions regarding lamps that were used in worship, and those same rituals were later carried over into the temple. One thing in particular is interesting about the way light was supposed to be handled in the temple. To me, it speaks to how we should operate now, in this time, if we want to git Lit, stay Lit, and Spread it.

When it came to handling worship, God was very serious about how it should be done. There's an entire book of the Bible, Leviticus, almost entirely filled with rules and regulations of how temple worship should be conducted. There were rules about the structure itself, the furniture in it, the tools that were used, everything right down to what the priests who served in the temple were allowed to wear. Every single one of these rules is explained in detail. They were put in place to set a standard and ensure that God's ways would not be forgotten.

You probably think your church has a lot of rules, but compared with this, probably not so much. There was an entire tribe of Israel, the Levites, completely dedicated to temple worship.

They were told specifically to study these rules and help the priests keep up with the tabernacle, and later temple worship. When a priest died, the new priest could only be selected from this tribe. It was an honor to be chosen to serve.

According to scripture, when the original altar for the tabernacle—God's portable temple—was built, the fire was lit with a thunderbolt of fire from heaven. In order to maintain this fire, the Levites and priests were supposed to continually feed it fuel. The idea was to create an eternal flame that would never go out. Since it was portable, there was even a plan in place for moving this fire. They would take hot coals from the altar, store them inside the Ark of the Covenant while they were marching.

Then those same coals would be placed on fresh wood and blown back to flame to start a new sacrificial fire. Wherever fire was used in the Tabernacle, for light, incense, or to burn sacrifices, it needed to come from this altar. . (Later, Solomon's temple in Jerusalem would have an altar that required the same kind of ritual tending.)

Then God told Moses, Tell Aaron and his sons exactly what I'm about to tell you. These are the rules for burning sacrifices in the Tabernacle. When you offer a burned sacrifice, it should stay on the altar overnight until morning but the fire has to keep burning the entire time.

Then a priest, dressed in linen from his undergarments out, needs to remove the ashes of the sacrifice from the altar and place them on the ground beside it. When they finish, the must immediately remove those clothes and change them. Once he is dressed again, the ashes have to be carried outside the camp to a place you have ritually cleansed.

This is important, they must not let the fire on the altar go out at any time. Every morning the priest should add fuel to the fire.

Then arrange a burned sacrifice over the fire and burn the fat as a fellowship sacrifice. Remember, the fire has to stay burning at all times, don't ever let it go out!

Moses' brother, Aaron, became the first priest. You might remember Aaron. He's the one who went with Moses to see Pharaoh, because Moses' had a speech problem—perhaps it was stuttering. He couldn't speak to the Pharaoh without feeling embarrassed.

After the ten plagues, and the Children of Israel's escape from Egypt, God gave the Ten Commandments on the mountain. Then after a big fundraiser to gather building materials, God tells Moses to build a tent. It was a kind of portable temple, called the tabernacle. This was where God's Spirit would live, right in the middle of the Hebrew camp. That's a pretty awesome thought, isn't it? The creative force behind the construction of the universe, is going to camp out right in town square where everyone can feel his presence. It must have been intense. God explains it all in Exodus 25.

God told Moses, "I need you to gather some things from the children of Israel. Don't force anyone to contribute, only those whose hearts are open and want to give. Here's what we need. We will need gold, silver, bronze, blue, purple and red yarn. We need fine linen cloth, goat skins, ram skins that are dyed with red dye. Also, any durable leather, acacia wood and olive oil. We'll use the olive oil for lamps.

Then we'll need spices for mixing anointing oil and perfume for incense. I also want you to gather up onyx and other gemstones for the priests' breast plates and robes.

When you have it all, I need them to build a meeting tent for me. I want to live in the camp with them. We'll call it the tabernacle, but it must be built exactly like I'm showing you.

From there, Moses recorded pages of instructions for everything in the tabernacle from the exact dimensions of the tent, to descriptions and measurements for the altar, lampstand, and every other tool they would need.

It was a massive undertaking. The Priests and Levites were important members of the camp because they spoke to and for God.

But here's what Jesus said about importance in God's Kingdom in Matthew 11. John the Baptist—Jesus' cousin—was in prison. He sent two of his disciples to ask Jesus if He was the messiah. After telling them to go and tell John that they had seen Jesus doing miracles and teaching, Jesus turned back to the crowd that was following him and said this.

John is the one the prophet Malachi meant when he said, "Pay attention, I'm sending a messenger to prepare the way for the Messiah"

But here's the truth, there's never been anyone born of a mother that is greater than John. Not one in the whole of human history. That being said, even the lowliest person in the kingdom of heaven is greater.

This tells us that we are more important even than the Old Testament priests; we ought to take it just as seriously when we worship a holy God. I'm not saying go out and get a jewel encrusted robe and start barbecuing livestock on an altar in your front yard, but I am suggesting that maybe there's more to us than we sometimes realize.

Bigger even than that, is what Paul makes clear in 1 Corinthians 3. He's talking about trial by fire, and we'll come back to that passage in Section 3 of this book. What I want you to see here comes in verse 16 as Paul compares the believer to this tabernacle system of worship. What the Israelites had as a nation —that relationship with God—is a model for what we have as individuals.

What don't you get? You are God's temple. His Holy Spirit lives inside of you. Think about it. If anyone destroys God's temple, won't God destroy him? God's temple is reserved for God's spirit, it is a holy space, and you are that tabernacle, you are God's home on earth.

We are God's temple. The same spirit that resided in flame and smoke in the Hebrew tent of meeting, lives in each of our lives. We are a reflection of Him.

What He told Moses to construct in bronze, gold, ram skins and linen, was nothing but a representation of the indwelling power of the Holy Spirit that was coming. In a way, it was God's proof of concept, a model to prove to man that their God could live side by side with them.

Back to Moses. Here's a fact you might not remember about this "fundraiser" God has him working on. They're in the desert. There's no city, no shops, no weavers, no looms. All they have is what they carried with them when they left Egypt, but God has a plan. Once Moses announces what they need, the people line up and begin to donate. Before they know it, they've collected more than they need. So much so, Moses eventually has to call off taking up the donations.

This to me is a super cool picture of how God prepares us and supplies us with what we'll need in order to do what He calls us to do. Before they left Egypt, the Egyptians had handed over much of their wealth to be rid of the Israelites, because they blamed them for the horrible plagues they'd been suffering.

So, all of the skilled crafts people among the Israelites gathered together and they built the golden and bronze implements, the curtains from goat skins and dyed them red. They carved designs into everything, and every single inch of this tent had meaning. All of it was a huge symbol of God and the Hebrews, and their relationship to each other, and ultimately a picture of God's desire to live in the hearts of his people.

You probably know at least a little about the most important part of the whole thing, which is the Ark of the Covenant. Some of you may not know what that means, until I say, Indiana Jones and the Raiders of the Lost Ark. If you remember the scene where the box is finally opened and the Nazis' faces are literally melted off, then you understand what we're dealing with here. This was the tent that was built to house this box, among other things.

When the Tabernacle is finally completed, and they're ready to open it for worship, Aaron and his sons are chosen to run things as the leaders of the tribe of Levi. There was this huge ceremony, and all the Hebrews were there to see it. The tabernacle was finally finished and it was being dedicated.

They lined everyone up, and Moses led Aaron through all of the rituals he'd need to know to offer sacrifices for forgiveness, and other things, and the people witnessed the entire event. You can imagine it was an exciting time. After hundreds of years in captivity in Egypt, the Hebrews were finally becoming their own nation, and God was going to live right there in the middle of their camp. Instead of the many gods of the Egyptians, they would all worship the One True God whom they'd known only as legend, passed down from their forefathers, Abraham, Isaac and Jacob.

So, Aaron's sons, Nadab and Abihu, were next in line to be priests. They decided, since there's nowhere in the Bible that anyone told them to do this, to offer incense on the altar. Moses had already given instructions about what they were supposed to wear and the tools they were supposed to use, and the exact recipe of the incense. But, either they were not paying attention, or, as some say, they may have been drunk. They got their incense burners ready, put on their priestly robes and before they headed in to the altar, they picked up something the Bible calls "strange fire," or "alien fire." There's some debate over what this means, but mostly it's agreed that they either lit the incense from some common campground fire, or they mixed the incense wrong.

I've also thought that perhaps the term strange fire refers not to where the fire came from, but the attitude with which it was presented. Instead of an act of worship, it was done out of a self-seeking motive, or perhaps haphazardly, as if it was just any other job. Whatever the case, it's clear that God was not pleased.

What happened next should serve as a warning to anyone reading this book.

Because, although I'm excited about teaching you all how to get lit for Jesus, stay lit and spread it to others, you have to remember this one point. Fire is not a thing. It's a chemical reaction and whenever heat, fuel, and oxygen combine in the right proportions, fire happens. That heat will then look for any fuel it can consume, whatever that fuel is. It might be an apartment building, or your house.

In the case of spiritual fire, there are all kinds of counterfeits, and we'll talk about that later. But understand this, anything that you get on fire for can consume you. If you get on fire for God, then God will sustain you, like the bush that didn't burn. Because He is the all consuming fire. But, if you allow yourself to think for one minute that this is about you, of if you forget that we are all following the example of a God who became a servant, or you take it upon yourself to make things happen, it can swallow you up.

Picture it like this. The Hebrews are all lined up, somewhere between two and four million people, all in their tribes, wearing their best clothes. Because remember, Egypt gave them gifts when they left, so this is no shabby crowd. And down through the camp, swinging their incense burners, come Nadab and Abihu. I picture it like a catholic priest with the incense burner coming down the aisle. If you've ever seen it in person, or you've seen it in a movie, you know it's a solemn deal.

As they get closer to the tabernacle, they must have been excited. Dad was a big shot and now, right here in front of all their countrymen, they were about to become a part of the family legacy. To me, it seems like their pride got in the way. Nearly everything else about this day is directed by Moses. The people have been working on this tent non-stop, and it's a big deal, but the Bible is completely silent as to where these two idiots got the idea to join in.

Now, the tabernacle has this huge curtain surrounding it on poles, creating a big courtyard inside, and any Hebrew in good standing, who has offered their sacrifices can come into this outer courtyard.

They sweep through it—incense burners held high. They walk past the altar, where dad has just burned a bull, past the huge bronze tub that the priests bathed in, and up to a second set of curtains surrounding the Holy Place.

There were some pretty specific instructions about this space. No one but a priest could enter it. So far, so good, Nadab and Abihu have been "sworn in" so to speak. Inside this area is a huge lamp, called the golden lampstand (which is where the modern Menorah is patterned after), and an altar for burning incense, which is where they're headed.

I picture these two clowns smirking to each other like a couple of frat boys who've made good. They raise the incense and swing it over the altar, sending the smoke up to heaven, the idea being that it creates a pleasing aroma for the presence of God. Everything you read about this ritual indicates it's a solemn, humbling thing, and shouldn't be done lightly. The priests were held to an impossibly high standard on their behavior and couldn't serve if they were in any way "unclean."

As Moses, Aaron, and the other priests look on, from the altar, comes the wrath of God in the form of fire, and instantly kills both of these two rebellious priests that had dared to offer "strange" fire on the altar. Their fried bodies are immediately taken out and buried.

Even this was covered by rituals, and the priests who picked them up would be considered "unclean" for even touching them to drag them out of the Holy Place, because they were dead. In fact, they had to go through a ritual bath and other ceremonies to get back into the Holy Place. God took it that seriously.

Now, I don't want to scare you. God isn't looking to strike you down and that's not what I'm saying. What I am saying is this. When you serve God, you need to make sure your hands are metaphorically clean.

You need to check your heart. We all have sin, but why are you serving Him? Is it for money, or fame? Is it out of some broken sense of obligation? Are you like Nadab and Abihu, just wanting to look like a bigshot?

Because if you're not serving willingly, out of love and a desire to sacrifice your own needs so others can meet Jesus, you might find yourself burned out, and we'll talk more about that later. Fire, in the wrong context, can be a scary thing But, for those who serve God openly and honestly, it holds no fear.

——————— *Chapter Four* ———————

VINDICATED BY FIRE

If we talk about fire in the context of living the Christian life and pretend it's only about spreading the gospel, we'd be doing some damage to the Bible's picture of the relationship between God and fire. There are two critical elements in the Bible narrative that have to be discussed when it comes to fire. One is purification, as we've just seen, the other is punishment.

When it comes to punishment and fire in my own life, I've spent a good bit of time avoiding being punished for fire, and even more fortunately, I've never been punished WITH fire. In my younger days I wasn't what you might call a "model citizen" when it came to playing with matches and in addition to the three stories I'm sharing in this book there are others that I might tell if we get that close. But nothing in my life can compare with the fire that Shadrach, Meshach and Abednego faced.

If there is anything I know for certain, it's that we'll all go through the fire of purification. However, God promises to sustain us. It's what comes out on the other side that He's interested in. In the case of Nadab and Abihu, there was nothing left. All of their work was deemed unworthy and utterly destroyed. God cut their lives short.

That's not always the case though. One thing that I think the Bible text does well is contrast. Generally, for every person that is evil and greedy, God paints a picture of one who is generous beyond reason. In contrast to the story of Nadab and Abihu, the self-serving sons of Aaron (say that three times fast), we're given a trio of young Israelites some generations later in the book of Daniel that not only faced fire, but were completely vindicated by it.

As Nadab and Abihu were tested and consumed in the purifying fire, there were three men whose story shows us what we can expect when the fire comes and we're truly Lit, staying Lit and working to spread it.

About three hundred years after David was bringing the ark up from Shiloh, the nation of Israel had fallen away from truly worshipping God. So, when King Nebuchadnezzar of Babylon attacked the city of Jerusalem in 605 BC, God gave them up. He handed them over to Babylon, as the prophets had told them would happen, and among those taken captive was Daniel.

You might remember Daniel if you spent any time in Vacation Bible School, Sunday School or church summer camp. He gets a lot of air time for surviving a sleepover with a den of lions, but that's a story for another time. Daniel served in the court of King Nebuchadnezzar because of his ability to interpret dreams. (Daniel's story is similar to what another young Hebrew, Joseph, did for the Pharaohs of Egypt.)

In fact, right before our story begins, Daniel had just gotten a promotion and you'd think Nebuchadnezzar would have learned his lesson, because God had spoken to him in dreams, but instead, he decided to set up a huge golden idol to himself about ninety feet tall. He had it set up on a plain called Dura and ordered that every official, from his right-hand man down to the dog catcher, should show up for a dedication ceremony. Then he had his heralds address the crowd.

Listen, O peoples of Babylon and all nations and languages gathered here! Here is what the king decrees! When the conductor strikes up the band, and you hear the music of the horn, pipe, lyre, trigon, bagpipe and the other instruments of this great orchestra, kneel! Bow down and worship this great image your king has set before you. Anyone who refuses to kneel, will be thrown into a furnace blazing with fire.

I'm sure you've faced peer pressure in your life to do things you didn't want to do, but this was a bit extreme. I don't know about you, but no one ever threatened to burn me alive if I didn't do what they said. I'd like to think that under that kind of pressure, I'd remain true to God; but if we're honest, I don't know if we can always say with one hundred percent certainty that we'd do the right thing. Especially not with the entire government watching and ready to carry out the threat.

So, the band cranked up and all across this great plain, thousands upon thousands of people as far as the eye could see, all knelt down, put their faces to the ground and worshipped Nebuchadnezzar's golden statue. I'm sure his ego was stoked. But not everyone went along with it.

To me, one interesting point here is this, who was the self-appointed punk that took it as their job to peek? I mean, here you are, on this giant field, and everyone is bowing. If your face is in the grass in worship, how do you have time to be looking around picking out those who refuse to comply. But we know those people in real life, and the always manage to find a way. In fact, people like this were the ones who'd gotten Daniel thrown to the lions, so evidently Babylon was filled with them.

The next thing I always think about is the courage it takes to stand up to something like this. There are people in this world who, unlike Nadab and Abihu, seem incapable of doing things out of a selfish motive. They do things, or refuse to do things, on principle—no matter the cost. Daniel's three friends, Shadrach, Meshach and Abednego were in that category.

In this case, it was the Chaldeans who ratted out our boys from Israel. Freaking Chaldeans, always stirring up trouble. So, they came to the king. As I picture Nebuchadnezzar, he's under some big pavilion tent on a hill overlooking this plain. Harem girls are serving him wine and grapes, and keeping him cool with ostrich feather fans like something out of a Cecil B. DeMille movie, like The Ten Commandments.

We aren't told the names of the Chaldeans, but I've got a pretty good idea of the oily, smarmy type of vermin they were. They approach the king's pavilion and the guards step in.

King, the Chaldeans are here to see you.

The king sighs. They irritate him too. But they also have good intel, so he waves them through.

This better be good, I'm late for my milk bath.

Well, King Nebuchadnezzar, your royal highness, protector of the realm, may you live forever...

Get on with it!

The king's aid leans in and reminds him.

Uh, sire, you ordered them to address you this way or be tossed into the furnace.

Oh, right, okay, whatever. Does it have to take so long every single time they say it?

The aid addresses the Chaldeans.

The king's in a hurry, can you say it faster?

Oh King Nebuchadnezzar, your royal highness protector the realm, may you live forever and your kingdom never end, if it pleases you sire, we've come with a report about the recent worship experience here on the plain.

Okay.

Oh King Nebu…

SPIT IT OUT MAN!

Well, sire, it seems that some of the Jews you put in charge in Babylon didn't exactly worship.

What do you mean, didn't exactly worship?

Well, they were seen standing, sire. Throughout the entire ceremony. They won't worship our gods and now it seems they refuse to bow down and you said anyone who doesn't bow down would be tossed….

Into the fiery furnace, I know I know! Say, doesn't your bother-in-law have the contract on stoking the fire in the furnace?

Well, King, your honor, sire, your excellency, I hardly see where that….

He does, doesn't he?

Yes sire.

You're a brown-noser and an opportunist. But, it does really tick me off that these Jews just don't seem to get it. In fact, I'm in the mood to roast a couple of Hebrew Nationals.

The more the king thought about it the angrier he got.

I mean, I go to all the trouble of commanding my treasurer to pay for this idol, and my chancellor for arts to commission the artist. I spent a week in negotiations to have the thing moved and set up, and the idol construction union raked me over the coals, so, you know what? Thank you for bringing this to my attention, you're right, they're just not paying enough attention to me. You can go.

The guards hustle out and bring the three Hebrews before the king. He's pacing he's so angry now.

I heard a rumor that you three ignored my direct order! Is it true? You know what, don't answer that, I know it's true. Someone saw you not doing what I told you to do. So, here's what I'm going to do. You three are Danny's friends, right? Well you're lucky I like him. But you three are a pain in my rear. So, here's what I'm going to do. Is the orchestra still here?

The king's aid has a quick whispered conversation.

Uh, yes, your highness, seems you threatened to throw them in the furnace, if they left the band stand before you gave the order. So, they are there.

Great! It's your lucky day! Here's what's going to happen. We're going out to the plain, and by we, I mean you three with my guards here, and when the band plays, you're going to worship. Refuse again and I'll toss you in the fiery furnace. Have you seen my furnace? You have, oh good, then I don't have to explain. Then we'll see if your God can deliver you from that!

Now go, I need my milk bath. Make sure they kneel! All the way, none of this halfway stuff!

42

What the king expected next was for these three to be hustled out, taught a lesson and brought back, ready to follow orders. But instead, they answered him back. A bad idea with a king.

King Nebuchadnezzar, we don't need to answer to you about our faith. If this is what you want, then the God we serve is big enough to rescue us from your furnace, as terrifying as it is and He will snatch us out of your very hand, king. But, even if He doesn't, understand this, King, we have made up our minds, and we won't bow down, or serve your gods, and we refuse to worship your golden idol.

That was the wrong answer. The king flipped out. He ordered the men to be marched directly to the furnace, and before they left, he directed the furnace tender to make the fire seven times as hot as it usually was. There would be no escape for the Hebrews.

The king ordered some of his strongest soldiers to bind the men in ropes and carry them to the furnace fully clothed in their robes and hats. In their hurry to get the blaze seven times as hot, the furnace was overheated and the soldiers that carried Shadrach, Meshach and Abednego died throwing them in.

It's in these moments right here, when the purifying fire is hottest that we find out what we're made of. Will we pass through the fire? Or like Nadab and Abihu, will the fire consume us and our work? For all their courage, this thought must have crossed their minds. Are we on fire for God, or just living like we're on fire?

After they'd fallen into the furnace, the king watched, expecting them to be consumed. The king didn't understand the nature of this fire. He thought he'd lit a consuming fire, but God's purification was taking place instead. As he watched dumbfounded, he saw something he didn't expect. He peered into the blazing furnace, confused.

Didn't we just toss three Hebrews in there all bound in ropes? Look!

Several of the officials looked, afraid to contradict the king, but were so shocked, they told him exactly what they saw.

What you say is true, but it looks like there are four men in the furnace, walking around free, completely unharmed, and the fourth looks like a son of the gods!

Nebuchadnezzar walked up as close to the furnace as he dared and shouted in to the three Hebrews.

Shadrach, Meshach and Abednego! Servants of the highest god, come out of the fire!

When the three men came out of the furnace, the officials gathered around them, but couldn't find a single scorch mark on them or their clothes. In fact, the only thing that had burned, was the ropes that bound them. They didn't even smell like fire.

After walking through the flames that the world designed to destroy them, the only thing consumed in the fire were the things that were binding them. The restrictions the world had put on them were gone, their false bondage to human expectation was destroyed, and God proved that their faith could stand the test.

Most of us will never face an actual fiery furnace. But, we all face testing in our everyday lives. Sometimes we feel the fire. God uses it to clean out and destroy attitudes and habits that aren't useful to building the kingdom. Other times we don't feel a thing. The attacks and accusations find no target in us and like Shadrach and company, we don't even smell like smoke!

As the king stands there with his governors and judges around him, he immediately does a 180 from his original position. Remember, he was insistent than anyone not worshipping his idol would be burned and it would be very tempting to just go along.

After all, God would understand, wouldn't He? But then these three guys would have missed out on hearing the king eat his own words.

> *The God of Shadrach, Meshach and Abednego is worthy of honor. He didn't just rescue them, but sent an angel to do it. These men have a lot of character. They knew what my decree was, but because they believed in their God so strongly, they ignored it for a higher purpose. They were willing to be roasted alive, rather than worship any other God.*

At this point, you're tempted to think the king finally gets it, ole Nebbie is finally leaving the dark side for the light, but what he says next kind of cracks me up and reminds me that sometimes people are still who they are, even after an encounter with God.

> *Here's what's going to happen. I'm passing a law, right now. Anybody, any nation, government or ethnic group that has anything bad to say about their God, should keep it to themselves, because if they don't, I'll personally see to it that they're ripped limb from limb and their houses are turned into piles of rubble. Because, I'm telling you, nobody's God rescues anybody like what we just saw.*

You have to give our boy points for his zeal, but I'm not really sure he understood the whole "Setting aside a people to bless the whole world," scenario that the God of Israel was going for. He continued to struggle with it throughout his story. In the next chapter, he makes a speech claiming to have basically built Babylon brick by brick with his own hands. But God gets the last word, when Nebuchadnezzar loses his mind and basically goes full werewolf, living in the woods like a beast until God's ready to restore him.

From our perspective, this story is amazing. Now, word of caution—never assume that God will save your bacon. There's one part of this story that many overlook when it gets shared, but the king got it.

These guys were prepared to burn. If you stick your neck out in this way, understand, you are performing on a high wire without a net. If you fall, God may choose to catch you, or He may allow you to be added to the long list of people who've died for their faith.

Our choice comes in either believing in a God who is big enough to save us from the fire or not. Our level of faithfulness and the fulfillment of God's plan will determine the rest. I don't know about you, but I want to live lit and sharing it so that I can say with confidence that my God will walk with me through any fire. I mean, it's hard to burn up in a fire when you were already "lit" when they threw you in!

—————— *Chapter Five* ——————

BACKSEAT BOTTLE ROCKETS

While the Great Tulsa Dumpster Fire of 1994 was a big deal and I should have learned my lesson, I didn't. Fast forward into my twenties and you'd find me playing with fire again. This time it had to do with bottle rockets.

As a lot of you may know my background is in music and I travelled a lot doing shows with bands. One of my longtime travel companions was a guy I'll call Bob, because he's a good guy and I don't want him linked into my shenanigans. So, Bob and I travelled all over the US and when we travelled, wherever we went, we carried bottle rockets.

If you're from Oklahoma, you probably just choked a little, because for over thirty years these have been completely illegal in a state where you can openly carry a firearm without a permit. The fine is about $1500, and you can go to jail just for having bottle rockets in some city limits. Regardless of this, we always carried them with us for one simple reason—they're a BLAST! Get it?

Over time we developed a game that we would play when we had any extra time. We'd find an abandoned piece of road, and lay the rockets on the ground. We'd get in front of them, light them, and then run. But not away from them. Too easy. We'd run in the direction the rockets were pointed!

It was awesome. Sometimes you'd get hit, sometimes they'd whiz past you, sometimes they'd veer off and explode behind you. No matter where they went, it was an adrenaline rush and we loved to do it every chance we got.

Out in the open, on a country road, the danger seemed fairly harmless. Even if you got hit, it would sting for a bit, but you'd survive, and most of the time you just got a heart pounding rush out of the deal. But I was never one to settle for a mere rush when I could look death right in the face. So, here's what I did.

Bob was driving on one of our trips; we were on our way to a buddy's apartment up I-35, the great mother road of Oklahoma. I'm sitting in the passenger seat getting fidgety and bored, so I looked around inside the minivan for something to play with. I spotted the fireworks bag. My gears started turning. I looked at Bob. He's focused on the road, so I stealthily slid my lighter out of my pocket and let my hand drag casually along the floor to the fireworks, drawing out a few bottle rockets.

Some of you see where I'm going with this, and I can hear you from here saying, "Oh no, you didn't!" And all I can say is, "Oh, yes I did."

Watching to see if Bob had noticed, I brought the rockets between my knees, hiding them from view and lit the lighter, letting the flame lick at the wicks. Several of them sizzled to life and I swung my arm back, dropping them into the floorboard, then sat facing straight forward, trying not to laugh, literally waiting for the fireworks to start.

The first rocket shot forward and under Bob's seat, sizzling, as sparks shot everywhere, then exploded with a bang! Meanwhile, Bob, hearing the rocket at his feet, picked his knees up and looked down, something you shouldn't do, while driving seventy miles an hour. By the time the second one hit the dash, we were almost over the line into the other lane on my side, and right outside my window was a big, ugly, mean looking biker on a hog that looked like it had seen a lot of road.

As the rockets began to explode in the van, I was laughing so hard, there were tears running down my face, and Bob is cursing me by this point. I reach over and pull the wheel back, taking us into our lane, but the rockets keep coming and Bob is veering all over by now, and the biker, who has been almost forced off the road, is pissed.

With tears streaming down my face, I turn to see Bob, face pale, eyes wide, white knuckles gripping the wheel as he checks his mirrors and comes up with one angry biker pulling in behind us. By now the guy is gunning it up on Bob's side and banging on his window with his fist, flipping the bird, as he screams a near constant stream of obscenity, and I'm just laughing.

Finally, the last rocket explodes and we're cruising along in a cloud of smoke, me laughing, Bob choking, as he rolls down the window and apologizes, but the biker isn't having it. Bob is back in control of the van by now and I suggest we speed up and lose the crazy biker. So, Bob pushes the pedal to the floor.

If you've ever tried to outrun a big road bike in a minivan, it's not a great idea, but through several lane changes, we felt we'd lost him. We took our exit and headed toward the apartment, only to find him in our rear-view mirror. Finally, through a series of turns, we seemed to be in the clear, so we proceeded to our destination.

By this time, Bob was reluctantly laughing, while also making it clear that if I ever did that again, I'm a dead man. I was still laughing. So, while Bob hustles inside to change his shorts, I started unloading the gear out of the van. I was just about done when I heard the rumble of road hog exhaust pipes and the hair on the back of my neck stood up. I looked over my shoulder, and there, fifty yards back and closing fast, is the biker from the highway and he's spotted me.

Had he not taken the time to kickstand his bike, I might not be writing this now because I'm pretty sure he was going to kill me.

Now I'm a big guy and I don't take off fast. Lucky for me he cared about his bike, because it gave me just enough head start to get inside the apartment, and he apparently didn't want to add home invasion to whatever record he already had, because he left shortly afterward.

Still to this day, I love fire. It can be fun to play with, but you've got to respect it. My disrespect for it that day nearly cost me a beating, and could have cost both our lives on the road. Sometimes God saves us from ourselves, but sometimes, he allows us to experience the consequences of our actions, even terminally. As a chemical reaction, fire happens and will keep happening until something interrupts the cycle. It's seen as both a tool and a dangerous force of nature.

As we've already seen in the story of Aaron's sons, the fire of God is no less dangerous than the physical thing. But, that's not the only time in scripture when the "fire of God" was not respected in a sense. Much later in the story of Israel, there was another time when God's instructions to Moses were not respected, and with fatal consequences. It happened just before the construction of Solomon's temple.

The Ark of the Covenant, containing manna from the desert, Aaron's rod that budded (even though it had been cut from the tree and should have been dead), and the original Ten Commandments written by the hand of God, had been taken away and kept in the home of a man named Abinadab at a place called Shiloh.

Now, there are some pretty strict guidelines for the use of fireworks printed on the package. I flaunted those that day in the van. I broke them hard, and it could have ended much worse. But when it comes to God's rules about how He wants to be worshipped, it's a lot more serious. Here's what was supposed to happen every single time the Ark got moved. First, from Exodus 25, God gave Moses instructions for setting it up to be moved.

Make four golden rings and fasten one on each foot of the ark, so that two are on each side. Make two long poles of acacia wood and plate them with gold. Then, slip the poles through the rings on the Ark to carry the ark with. Do not remove these poles from the ark.

It's pretty clear, isn't it? They set this thing up to be moved by carrying. Not sure why it mattered, but if God says something matters, it matters. The poles served a couple of purposes. First, they allowed the Ark to be lifted without touching it. This was very essential. In fact, God's instructions included the dire warning that anyone who touched it in the wrong way, without expressly being designated by God, would die.

Secondly, it was the easiest way to allow more than two people to lift this heavy box and march with it, since it had to be moved, sometimes daily, over long distances and rough terrain. It was a pretty practical solution, and if you've ever seen a movie where a troop of explorers march a long distance, you'll notice that system is still used for carrying heavy boxes to this day.

Then we get this from Chapter 4 of the book of Numbers, regarding the preparations and procedure of moving the tabernacle and its sacred elements. First, a specific group of Levites, one family basically, the Kohathites, were the only ones supposed to be involved. Here's what God told Moses.

Moses, tell the Kohathites that their one and only job in my meeting tent is to care for the most holy things. Whenever it's time to move camp, Aaron and his sons, and them only, should go into the Holy of Holies (the innermost sanctuary reserved for the high priests only) and take down the curtains that shield the people from my presence. Lay that curtain over the Ark. Cover this curtain with a heavy leather cover, then a solid blue cloth on top of that and put the poles in place.

This was just the prep work, before the Kohathites could even pick this thing up. And again, the warning was that anyone who deviated from this plan, would get cooked.

51

I'm sure in the early days, when the smell of burning priest was still fresh in their memories, those who followed Aaron's sons in service worked hard to get it right. But time makes people forget.

When King David took the throne in Jerusalem, he was excited about restoring proper worship.

To do that, they needed to establish the sacrifices they'd followed in the desert. So, he went to Abinadab's house where the Ark had been stored, to pick it up. He invited over 30,000 able bodied young men to go with him.

The Bible says they build a new cart to carry it back. While it doesn't explain this, I've always thought maybe this was a sign of respect, but not the respect God wanted, as you'll see in a minute. Here's what we're told in 2 Samuel Chapter 6. Everything was going pretty good until they reached a bump in the road.

As the cart reached the edge of the stone floor where Nakon sorted his grain, the oxen stumbled. Uzzah, one of the sons of Abinadab, reached up to steady the Ark. Because they'd ignored his instructions and treated the Ark with such disrespect, God struck Uzzah and he died right there, beside the cart.

It was a full three months of prayer and waiting for God to speak before David tried again and successfully moved the Ark to Jerusalem. This time they carried it with poles like Moses had instructed, and every six steps, just to be sure, they sacrificed a bull. David wasn't taking any chances with the fire of God breaking out again.

From sacrifices, to cleansing, to light, when we look back through the Bible, nearly everywhere we look, God is using fire as a personal symbol. When Adam and Eve were removed from the garden, the angel's sword was set on fire.

When Moses met God in the wilderness, it was in a burning bush that wouldn't go out, and later, when God etched the Ten Commandments in stone on top of a mountain, the mountaintop appeared to be consumed with fire.

What starts out as a warning and a judgement becomes a comfort though, when the Hebrews follow Moses into the wilderness and God shows up as a "pillar like cloud" in the daytime and a "pillar of fire" at night, to let them know they are safe. When the cloud or fire stopped, they camped. When it moved, they followed.

All throughout scripture, lamp, light, and fire are intertwined, and almost everywhere you see it, it is a symbol for God, or God's Spirit.

After thinking about fire for all of these years, I've come to this conclusion. It's more viral than viral marketing. What's cool is that the fire we're talking about—the Bible kind of fire that represents God and God's Spirit—lives in us as believers. But how does it get there?

This book is my best attempt at explaining that. It's a manual, of sorts, on how to apply this teaching and take actions, because I firmly believe that action changes things. Belief, for the sake of belief, not so much. So, in the next couple of pages, I'm going to share with you the passages I'll be using in this book to teach you how to Get Lit, Stay Lit, and Spread it.

I know from my first book that readers really like Bible stories, so I'll be going into each of these passages in detail further on. But for right now, let's build a foundation of basic understanding. Sound good?

While I'm all about fire in its wild natural state, there are times when I'm in awe of it in its smallest forms. If you have never been to a candlelight Christmas Eve service, you need to go. I'm just telling you straight up, it may seem like the dorkiest thing you can think of, but it's not. Why?

Well, first of all, it's Christmas. And a candlelight service is like the super bowl of Christmas. Of course, Jesus is the main attraction, but next comes the awesome beauty of the candlelight service.

Imagine singing in a darkened room as first one candle, then two, then four, then eight are all lit. Then sixteen and thirty-two until hundreds, or even thousands, of tiny flames are dancing across the room. All around you there are smiles lighting up as the candles light their faces, until the whole room is lit with a soft, dancing glow. This is how it works in the Kingdom of Heaven.

From one soul to the next, to the next, until as far as the eye can see, there are souls burning bright for Jesus, each person touching other lives, until they catch it too. And that fire, the same fire we're spreading, life-on-life now, is an unending chain of one person telling another, all the way back to the people Jesus was speaking to when He said this in John Chapter 8.

I am the light of the world. Whoever follows me will never walk in darkness, but will have the light of life.

This was that first spark. The original source of the heat of the fire of the gospel. Right here in this verse. The light that Isaiah prophesied was sparking a fire in every heart that had fuel to burn; and it's burning to this day. Unlike the Great Tulsa Dumpster Fire that I started, no empire, no government, no religion, no philosophy, has ever been able to extinguish the Gospel flame. And now you have become the keeper of the flame.

Jesus made no distinction between Himself and us on this issue. In fact, He greatly elaborates when it comes to our role in spreading the light. Remember, I told you this was what God was about from the very beginning. Bringing light into this world is a big deal to God and now it's our job. Here's what Jesus had to say about it in Matthew 5.

You are the light of the world.

Here is the interesting part. He was speaking to a whole mountainside full of people. It wasn't a private-invitation-only event. He didn't say this just to his apostles, or a ministry committee, or a pastors' conference.

It wasn't an elitist message. He was talking to farmers, and fishermen, and housewives. They were merchants, and carpenters, and children. Grandmothers, babies, and teens, and at least one former tax collector. You are the light of the world.

He goes on to say,

A city built on a hill cannot be hidden. Neither do people light a lamp and put it under a bowl. Instead, they put it on its stand, and it gives light to the whole house.

So often, I think we get hung up on the light imagery here and miss the introduction of the Kingdom of Heaven. A City on a Hill filled with light! What an amazing picture. But Jesus doesn't just stop there. No. He has expectations for us, and he believes in our ability to carry out the mission of "Let there be light."

In the same way, let your light shine before others, that they may see your good deeds and glorify your Father in heaven.

And there it is. Perhaps the clearest and most concise of His calls to action.

Get lit: Let your light shine.

Stay lit: Do good works. Meaning, love God. Stay close to him, build relationship, fuel yourself up through His Word, and love people.

Spread it: That others may see you, your passion for Jesus, and your deeds that glorify god.

Jesus doesn't just tell us how spreading the gospel works, but he defines what it means to be lit. It's right here: Let your light so shine before others, that they may see your good works. Throughout his ministry, He worked hard to make sure we knew what we were supposed to be about. Love God and love people. When you do that, it naturally leads you to good works.

Let there be light!

In another passage, his cousin John the Baptist, gives us a deeper glimpse into this process when he says about Jesus in Matthew Chapter 3.

I baptize you with water for repentance. But after me comes one who is more powerful than I, whose sandals I am not worthy to carry. He will baptize you with the Holy Spirit and fire.

Talk about getting lit! A baptism of fire! This phrase is so amazing that it's almost become a cliché. When people talk about a baptism of fire, they mean an experience that not only initiates them into something, but tests them, and burns things off that they don't need. Just like Shadrach, Meshach, and Abednego were set free from their bonds.

This event, this baptism of fire, not only gets you lit, it prepares you to light others, which is the whole point of the exercise. Without that, we'd just be a "Candle in the Wind" like the Elton John song, "Never knowing what to cling to when the rain set in." But, instead, we're a part of a great city on a hill whose light cannot be hidden! Isn't that exciting? The world is filled with people looking for a place to belong and Jesus just declares that His followers have their own community.

Chapter Six

GET LIT

Let's recap. So far we've covered the connection between fire and light, we've seen how people show up when there's fire, and we've discovered that Jesus offers to baptize us with fire. But what does that look like? Are all fires the same? Are Christians the only ones who get "Lit"?

To answer this question honestly, I have to say No. Before you argue, hear me out. To be lit, in my opinion, is any attitude that's contagious and spreads among likeminded people. And we've all heard the world's version of lit, haven't we? In fact, it seemed like there were a couple of years there where every song on the radio was talking about it! I think Ludicris said it best in his song, "Get Lit".

> *Ima drink until I'm drunk, smoke until I'm high*
> *Hustle till I ball, get money till I die*
> *These haters want my paper and the snakes is out to get me*
> *So when I leave I'm taking everything with me*

And, if I'm honest, there was once a big part of me that had that exact same attitude. Lit, in the world's eyes, is one big party. It's drugs, alcohol, a sexual free-for-all, and with no responsibilities. We all know people like this. To some of you, that may sound pretty attractive, and I totally get it. The party scene was fun! For a while.

But, just because you're sober, doesn't mean you're not lit in the ways of the world. Many people sober up, but fail to find real purpose. They turn their lit attitude toward other things. I would say a lot of the world's extreme athletes are definitely lit! They ignite something in others too! It's inspiring to see them conquer their fears and push the boundaries of human endurance. But, without love for their fellow man, and a connection to the source of the light of the universe, that's strange fire.

We don't call them Hollywood stars for nothing. They burn bright, don't they? It's easy to get caught in the glow of their light and mistake it for something real. That's not to say there's no one in Hollywood worth looking up to. Some of them do great work in their communities and the larger world, but the fire they burn with is a fire that originated here on earth, in the land of the shadow of death. Someday their work will end. That strange fire will consume it all, as it's divided among those who are left when they leave this life.

Recently, we've been exposed to what some in our financial markets are up to behind the scenes, but if you see them in their day-to-day, they are lit! They wear the best clothes, drive the nicest cars, live in the plushest houses, eat at the best restaurants. Life is pretty sweet. And, you can have that too, if you're willing to burn with their type of fire. But it's often mixed with greed and hatred for those they consider less than themselves.

But, what did Jesus say about this? "The love of money is the root of all evil!" (1 Timothy 6:10) So, what did he mean? Was he talking about wanting to be successful? Well, no, not entirely. He was talking about wanting success, so that you can spend it all on your own selfish desires. And he explains that. When we get wrapped up in material things, so much so that we forget God and the other people with whom we share this planet—beyond our own immediate circles— we're burning, but it's strange fire and it will consume us.

And for the believer, it's hard to have enough balance to be lit in those ways. In fact, Jesus said that you can't serve everything this world has to offer and God at the same time. Because, everything we own can easily own a piece of us, and we become a slave to getting and maintaining that lifestyle (whatever that lifestyle is). He said you cannot serve two masters, because in your heart, you will love one and hate the other, that you cannot serve both God and money. (Matthew 6:24)

And you're thinking, Come on, Kelly. Surely Christians don't have the secret sauce when it comes to doing good and loving our fellow man! I hear you, and I agree! In fact, there's hardly a day goes by, I don't see someone who has no interest in God, being a better "Christian" than some of the professing Christians I know. We certainly are not perfect and there are many people out there who are doing the right thing. I have to agree with Paul who said that love does not rejoice in unrighteousness, but rejoices with the truth! (1 Corinthians 13:6) The name on the door often has no bearing on how much love is poured out inside. If the world is doing good, we shouldn't protest; we should be joining them!

In every age there have been great moral teachers, men and women who understood truth and the principles of God, but didn't get it from the Bible. Many of them didn't, or don't, even believe in a creator. How is this possible? Because God didn't say we were the only light in the world.

No, we're told over and over that creation speaks of the creator, that it echoes God. And Christians are not the only ones that can hear it. Not by a long shot. But what we're told is that we are a part of a city whose foundations are not laid by hand. That God is building something that transcends this world. This is what sets us apart. Our light is not just for this life, like so many other positive, good philosophies, but it speaks of a life to come. We're not trying to escape into that future, but we are preparing to be citizens of a kingdom with supernatural foundations.

Paul spoke of people who "had a form of godliness, but denied the power in it." When we include God in our good works, it's amazing how much further it can go.

We are not limited to just what we can do in our own power. When we get lit in partnership with the Creator of the universe, He can magnify our efforts many times over—just like Jesus with the loaves and fishes—multiplying it by lighting one life, by one life, by one life, until, instead of one good man or woman, there is an army of followers of Jesus, ready to do the good works that God prepared for us before the beginning of the world.

You see, there is a big difference between "being on fire," and "living like you're on fire." A person who is on fire, with the baptism of fire Jesus promised, is sustained. But doing it all under your own strength, is a recipe for disaster. Like I said, we need to applaud and help those who are willing to do good work, regardless of their beliefs. But if you watch long enough, anyone who lives like they are on fire, will eventually burn themselves out, with very little hope of getting lit again.

Take party lit for example. The human body can only sustain so much damage, and night after night, week after week of partying hard, is literally like being on fire. It feels great and makes you think you are on top of the world, but soon comes the crash. When that happens, all of those people who lifted you up will walk away. No one wants to stick around a burned-out shell of a human being. Except Jesus, that is.

If you remember reading in my first book, my time of living like I was on fire ended with me skidding down a highway in a horrible car wreck that stripped most of the skin off my back and left me in a burn unit, fighting for my life. This is what I'm talking about. Hopefully God won't need to go to such extremes to get your attention, but trust me when I say, He's not as concerned about getting you there comfortably, as He is in getting you there, period. He will if He has to.

If you're lit on your own energy and physical exploits, it's no mistake that they call it a crash-and-burn when you end up crippled by the injuries, aging out of your lifestyle, or just being overshadowed by the next latest and greatest player of the game.

No matter how fit you are, no matter who trains you, what your mental game is, what your nutrition plan pumps into you, that fire can only burn so long. Since you are the only fuel it's got, and then it will die down to a smolder, and eventually wink out altogether.

The wealthy, in their lit lifestyle are constantly having to reinvent themselves just to keep it interesting. Many turn to sex, drugs, crime, or the adrenaline high of risking their lives just to prevent boredom. This kind of achievement lasts only so long and a big part of the high is the attention of others, which has to be constantly maintained.

As for the people who are on fire with love for their fellow man, this is more sustainable. But we all know people who wear themselves out as volunteers. We've all heard stories about people who work full time jobs just to run some type of non-profit, and without the sustenance that comes from a place that is bigger than they are, over time, they too burn down to the wick and fade out in a puff of smoke.

But the fire of God is a nourishing fire. We get this all consuming fire by having an encounter with Jesus Christ! When this happens, when you seek to know God with all your heart, He will draw near to you. (James 4) And when that happens, it will truly set you on fire like you've never been before.

The brighter we burn, the more is poured into us. But, beyond that, this "work" isn't a solo sport. Everywhere you look in the New Testament, there is all of this inclusive language about community.

They were together, in one accord. They sold all they had and gave to those in need. They were not just there for themselves, and they were not just there as themselves. This can sometimes be a hard adjustment for Americans, with our die-hard individualism. God's kingdom is a place for neighbors and brother's keepers. It just is.

There's a lot of talk in the Word about self-sacrifice, because this is a long game. It's a marathon, not a sprint, and beyond that, it's a relay.

You will be handing off this work to the next generation. It's not a thing you will ever see to completion, because even if the Kingdom was fully realized right now, there would still be work to do.

Besides the community of support and the sustenance of the Holy Spirit, your work and your fire is designed to outlive you. You get as far as you get. You help light as many other lights as you can. There are no quotas. And then, when your shift is over, you hand it off to the next crew. Just like you picked up where those before you left off—so it will be for your children and their children. Your work and fire lives on in the lives you've touched, and the lives those lives touch, which goes on until the end of this age.

That's why it's so critical that we learn how to stay lit! There is nothing that sets back the Kingdom worse than burnout. So many times we see people who get on fire, and stay on fire, until they reach a certain age, and then they smolder. But we'll get into that later.

So, what is meant by "Get Lit"? What are we talking about? Is it just another way of saying you need to get saved? No. It's the step beyond that. It's not just about getting your ticket punched for the heaven express; it's about finding so much passion in your walk with Jesus that you begin to duplicate yourself. Make disciples. Because without that, how can we ever bring more light?

Lit is the person who cannot help but help when they see someone in need. Lit is the person who plans their life around being able to pour into the lives of others, not just in church but everywhere they go. Lit is the person who works hard on themselves, not just so they can please God, who already loves them, but so they can be of the most use to their fellow man!

Lit is the Good Samaritan, who saw a man who could have been his enemy bleeding on the side of the road and not only took him to a hospital, but paid for it and offered to take care of any other expenses if there were any.

Lit is when people look back on your life and say, "They loved not their own lives even unto death." Because remember, eleven of the twelve apostles were killed as martyrs not for fame or glory, not for some political empire, but because they believed in Jesus' vision of the Kingdom of Heaven. Hebrews says, they "Longed for a better country." (Hebrews 11:16) A new way of life, a world where people acted out of love, rather than greed.

They wanted it so badly, and believed in their cause so strongly that their own lives became secondary to the kingdom.

Lit is what the Apostle Paul was talking about as he examined death and said, for me to Live is Christ, to die is gain. (Philippians 1:21) Because he knew that his own personal gain would be greater if he left this life, but he believed that his work in this life was worth more than that.

Lit, for you, is going above and beyond where you've been with Jesus. It's seeing growth in parts of yourself you never even knew existed. It's learning to love in new ways that make you question if you ever knew what love was to begin with. It's serving in positions that don't necessarily excite you, not because some church program needs it, but because you see what it's doing to benefit others and you just have to be involved.

That's why I'm so excited about what I'm going to share with you through this book. It's maybe the single greatest realization I've made, beyond realizing I needed to get right with God. If Reckless Love Revolution, is the invitation to the dance, this is the moves, baby, this is what it's all about. It's how we achieve the vision of RLR in real time, in the real world, with real people. And it matters now more than ever.

There's this really cool passage that I think fuels this idea for me. It's in Romans. Paul is talking about how whatever we suffer in life can't compare to the things God wants to reveal to us. And then it says this in Chapter 8.

> *In fact, all creation is eagerly waiting for God to show who his children are. Meanwhile, creation is confused, but not because it wants to be confused. God made it this way in the hope that creation would be set free from decay and would share in the glorious freedom of his children.*

This right here, is what getting lit is all about. As we share the fire of God in our own lives, so bright that it sparks others, we are a part of this project that reveals who the sons and daughters of God truly are. And why? Because God wants to set his creation free from decay so they can share in our freedom! Isn't that amazing?

If you thought some great afterlife was all this was about, you are wrong! We are on a mission that was started with Jesus' birth, and His death on the cross, to redeem creation back to God. If there's anything more worth living for, I challenge you to show it to me.

SECTION TWO - STAY LIT

Chapter Seven

THE FIRE TRIANGLE

If you've ever watched "Survivor" you might be tempted to believe that getting a fire started is all there is to survival. Once it's burning, you're good to go. But if you've ever watched the survivalist show "Alone" you know that keeping that fire going is the real trick. Because the universe will throw everything at you to make that fire go out, and it's the only thing standing between you and the vicious predators waiting to lick your bones clean.

From wind, to rain, to lack of fuel, to the exhaustion that sets in finding, hauling and chopping that wood—it's hard. But, if you've seen either show, then you also know that those who manage it are so much better off than those who let it go out. Also, it's much harder to get it going once it's dead. Fire is life.

It is the single biggest factor on both of these programs in people giving up early, checking out and quitting before the game is finished, or their survival time is up.

It provides a way to purify water; cook food; heat the body; and keep insects, and more dangerous animals, at bay, that nothing else can replace. Once it's gone, or if it never gets established, morale slips, emotions start to get ragged, and you watch as once strong competitors slowly slip toward the edge of mental breakdown.

The same thing is true in the Christian life. You can basically trip over a Bible and fall into a relationship with Jesus. Especially in the Bible belt, where I live, there's a church on every corner. Finding someone to help you meet Jesus is easy. But making it a vital, growing thing that lights your world and influences others to engage with Jesus, is another process altogether. Many times, the same people who helped you find Jesus don't even know the secrets we're sharing here. The sad part is, it's all in the Bible!

There's nothing I share here, or have ever shared, that hasn't been lying around, waiting to be discovered inside those leather-bound covers for two millennia. I didn't invent any of this. I'm not even really innovative in the way I share it. I'd like to think I was, but it's all pretty basic. I think this is why the Bible speaks to our connection with the infinite, our relationship to the divine creator, as a personal thing. It's something that takes place inside the hearts and minds of believers.

It's why those who've followed the path of contemplative Christianity, like Monks, have often come to such deep understandings. Even then, if they didn't take the time to come back to the world, publish their revelations and share what they learned, it would die with them. It would do us no good. All of the elements have to be put in place, eventually, to make fire.

That fire—that lasting connection with God that we talked about in section one of this book—is vital. Make no mistake, there are predators who would love nothing better than for your fire to go out.

People who'd like to discredit your faith, political forces that would love to have you on their side instead of standing for what's right, and finally, a spiritual force that opposes believers in their attempts to get lit, stay lit and spread it.

That, I think, is one of the biggest reasons that God, in His wisdom, exists in three persons. That third person, the Holy Spirit, or the Spirit of God in the Bible, is the One this section of the book is mostly about. Without the indwelling of every believer by the Holy Spirit of God, Satan would have no trouble snuffing us out.

Think about it. How hard is it to discourage a human? Sometimes all it takes is a single word, or even a facial expression, without a single word. We're so fragile. And that's over real world issues that we can see, taste, feel, smell, and experience in a measurable way. So, how much harder would it be for us to maintain a connection with an ethereal, esoteric, spirit force that's as different from our everyday experience as night is from day, without some kind of connection?

Tada! Introducing the Holy Spirit. That Holy Spirit is often referred to as the third person of the trinity—misunderstood, sometimes ignored, and some denominations even pretend like He doesn't exist anymore. Seriously, some people treat the Holy Spirit, like he's the Ringo Star of the Trinity. Oh sure, He's in the band, but is he really a part of it all?

To me, the Holy Spirit represents the fire that comes into every believer's life when they meet Jesus. In fact, John the Baptist was one of the first to describe it that way. John was an interesting dude. He was the last of a dying breed: the Old Testament prophets. By Biblical standards, he was the greatest of them all. In fact, Jesus even says in Matthew 17, that he's the second coming of Elijah. More about Elijah at the end of this section, and I think you're going to like it.

But John was a radical. I'm not talking about his politics, either. I mean, literally, the man lived a radically different lifestyle. From his fashion choices, to his hermit living arrangements out in the wilderness, to his diet, John was weird. Not only that, but he was one of those guys who just didn't care what you thought, as long as God was on his side. In fact, it got him killed. Beheaded, to be exact.

That's another story. Before he called out the king and lost his head to a bratty princess's birthday wish, John was preaching along the Jordan River. The Jordan was pretty significant to the Jews. It was the line between their journey from Egypt and their arrival in the Promised Land. John was sent to prepare the way for Jesus by preaching a higher moral standard and a message of repentance from abusive behavior and misusing others.

The Jews often used baptism as a ritual symbol of cleansing, and John was baptizing people by the river Jordan. One day, while John is preaching, his cousin Jesus shows up with some of his crew and asks John to baptize Him. It wasn't a random happening. In fact, it had been prophesied in the Old Testament. But even as cocky as John was, he was nervous about basically baptizing God. I kind of get it. Dunking the Messiah would be a big deal. You wouldn't want to mess that up.

"Listen, this isn't how this should go," John says. (I'm paraphrasing here.) "I should not be baptizing you, cousin, you should be baptizing me. And I think we both know it."

Jesus smiles. "Listen, this is what Dad wants. So, we're going to look past how awkward this feels and you're going to just accept this honor, okay?"

So, he does.

But, it's something John says right before Jesus shows up to get baptized that I want to focus on. It's in Matthew chapter three.

"Oh, sure, I baptize you with water, and this will forgive your sins because you've repented, but I'm telling you, there's someone coming that has more to offer. He will baptize you with the Divine Spirit of God and Fire!"

It's so cool how themes are repeated over and over again throughout scripture. It's like God wants to make sure even us slow pokes understand it.

Here is John, sharing with us, in case we weren't sure already, that God is a fire. Not only that, but He exists in a form that will be fire, inside of every single believer. That's awesome!

This Holy Spirit and fire is a metaphor when John says it, but if we fast forward a little bit, we see that John is foretelling an actual event on the day of Pentecost. We find it in the second chapter of Acts, a chapter that has so much crammed into it about the birth of the church it's amazing. I think I see something new every time I read it.

Here's the scene. Jesus is dead. Not only dead, but resurrected and then sucked up into heaven with everyone watching, like something out of a Spielberg film. The disciples are struggling. They had just replaced Judas (who hung himself), with Matthias so there would still be twelve apostles to help lead this new movement. So, the disciples are in the upper room, waiting for the Helper Jesus has promised them. They're praying along with a crowd of other believers, when this wind suddenly starts up inside the house!

Here's what it says.

They were all together in one place on the day of Pentecost, when a sound like a huge a wind came up. As they looked, what looked like flames of fire appeared, and separated so that a flame rested on each of them. Then, the Holy Spirit filled them and they each started speaking in different languages!

What? Can you imagine that scene? Talk about getting lit! Lit-erally. (See what I did there?) Wind inside the house, a big rushing flame that divides and enters every person? Sounds like a scene from a horror movie or something, except in this case, the world was about to be changed for the better!

So, what does this spooky scene have to do with us?

Well, Paul tells us later, in Romans chapter 8 that we are no longer in the physical realm as believers, but the Spirit of God lives in us. In fact, he says it's true for every single follower of Jesus and that if the spirit isn't in you, you're not of Christ. Pretty strong words.

That's the same spirit that showed up as wind and fire on Pentecost in Acts chapter two. The same exact thing happens to you, whether you feel anything, speak in foreign languages, or not. Jesus promised it would in John Chapter 16 when He tells the disciples it's better for them if He leaves, because He's sending a Comforter to walk with them. Pretty awesome.

I can remember when I was young, thinking it would be so cool to actually meet Jesus. You know? To hear Him preach and watch Him heal people and do the Stuff. But, here's the man Himself telling us that that's not the best thing. That those who died before his crucifixion actually missed out as far as life on Earth was concerned, because having the Holy Spirit indwell us is better than Him being here with us! Incredible!

What an aid to staying lit, to have the actual creative force of the universe live in you. We don't have to imagine that, it's our reality. But somehow, we manage to forget that there's also things for us to do to maintain that connection. That's what this second part of the book is about. Remembering who we are, and finding ways to engage the divine so that our fire will stay burning brightly and not die out.

Even with the indwelling wisdom of the ages on my side, sometimes my finite mind just doesn't get it. When I started thinking about being on fire, staying lit and spreading it in relationship to being a Christian, I couldn't quite figure the analogy. So, God did what he does sometimes and told me to "Google it."

"What?"

"Just Google it"

Now, this might seem a bit sacrilegious to say this, but God is constantly telling people to find inspiration in the things around them. In Proverbs, Solomon records that we should watch ants to learn about hard work, He told Job to ask the animals about Him, and Jesus told us to look at lilies and sparrows for inspiration on how to trust God. So, I don't suppose it's so far-fetched to use Google.

So, I did, I typed in, "How to stay on fire" because essentially, at the end of the day, that's what I want to know! If I get on fire for Jesus, the last thing I want to do is burn out. And the first thing that popped up was the Wikipedia page for the fire triangle.

The Fire Triangle or Combustion Triangle is a simple model for understanding the necessary ingredients for most fires.

The triangle illustrates the three elements a fire needs to ignite: heat, fuel, and an oxidizing agent (usually oxygen). A fire naturally occurs when the elements are present and combined in the right mixture, meaning that fire is actually an event rather than a thing. A fire can be prevented or extinguished by removing any one of the elements in the fire triangle. For example, covering a fire with a fire blanket removes the oxygen part of the triangle and can extinguish a fire. In large fires where firefighters are called in, decreasing the amount of oxygen is not usually an option because there is no effective way to make that happen in an extended area.

Right there in black and white was so much information I couldn't believe it. My mind immediately started filling in the blanks. First, I noticed something. This triangle, like so many things that are triangular in shape, requires all three sides to be in place in order to exist. If you remove just one side, or even shortchange it a little, fire will not happen.

For instance, if the spark is just too small to provide the required heat, no fire. If the fuel isn't plentiful enough, won't burn, or is wet, no fire. And if you don't have enough oxygen, no fire. Any of these three could also be removed from a raging fire to immediately suppress it. This made a lot of sense to me.

See, I've never thought that following Jesus was just about one thing. Going to church doesn't make you a disciple, neither does telling people, or just being a good person. It takes all of the spiritual disciplines (disciple—discipline) to create the triangle. Without all of these things firing on all cylinders, you're not going to get far in building the kingdom, or reaching people with the light. How could you? Your fire is either sputtering, or out completely. So, how could I make this clear?

———————— Chapter Eight ————————

FIRE NEEDS TO CONSUME OXYGEN

I started thinking about what this chart would look like if instead of the chemical reaction that causes most fires, it represented how to get lit for Jesus, stay lit, and spread the fire to others. It didn't take long to get the first two. They seemed fairly obvious to me. Of course, I'm not saying God didn't just reveal it to me, but the pieces came together almost right away.

Heat, or a source of ignition, was the first thing that caught my eye. We've gone over this a lot in the first part of this book. I thought back to the fires I'd started and the analogy seemed clear. The flame, the spark, the source of heat in a Christian life is the source of life, God the Creator, His Spirit and our connection to the infinite divine through Jesus.

That spark exists without me. It's there and available to anyone willing to access it. But when it comes to building God's Kingdom, the spark on its own can't create fire. I know it sounds wrong to say that God can't do something, but the truth is He created it this way. It's His system and He did it for a purpose. He created us for relationship with Him. So, He builds His kingdom in a way that gets us involved. He needs us to build this kingdom.

Fuel also seemed like a no brainer. It's not quite as easy as saying, "Read your Bible," but you've got to be inspired by something to walk the walk. It's not always easy. The other half of that was: you have to apply the fuel. As long as the fuel and the spark are kept apart, there is no fire. Anyone who has used a gasoline engine gets the basic gist of this. But if not, think of it this way. Would you be afraid to have a box of matches on a shelf over your firewood storage? Of course not. In fact, many people may be thinking, "Hey, that's what I've got right now."

As long as those matches remain in that box, there's zero chance of them lighting a fire with that wood. In fact, I'd go further. You could set that matchbox on the wood itself and you still wouldn't have fire, even though in an oxygen-rich environment, everything you need for a fire is present. You could take the match out, and lay it on the log! Watch out! It's getting dangerous now. No, it's not. Without you taking action to strike that match, it remains a potential source of heat, but it cannot create fire on its own.

All along the way there are actions we need to take to make this process what it is. The Bible says we don't have any part in saving ourselves, but it is filled with examples of how we must take action to fully engage as believers. We are commanded over and over to love, pray, feed, help, minister to, and carry each other's burdens. This is a partnership. It's not just us serving Him, or Him building a playground for us. We're a critical part of His mission.

At this point I had a basic understanding of the spark and fuel legs of the triangle but when I got to oxygen, it just wasn't clicking. Since I felt like God was leading me down this path. I knew there was a road sign, or something I was missing. I went back over the other two, but nothing seemed to fit. I think sometimes things are hard for us so we'll actually search ourselves. Looking inside to the Spirit that lives within each believer is a good practice, and sometimes God doesn't provide the answers in the outside world.

I struggled and struggled, then it occurred to me that maybe God had already answered me when he told me to Google it. Finally I went back to Wikipedia and there it was. I don't know why I hadn't seen it before.

A fire can be prevented or extinguished by removing any one of the elements in the fire triangle. For example, covering a fire with a fire blanket removes the oxygen part of the triangle and can extinguish a fire. In large fires where firefighters are called in, decreasing the amount of oxygen is not usually an option because there is no effective way to make that happen in an extended area.

Did you get that? Did you really see what it says there about big fires? Because when I did, I got excited. And it led me to the discovery I'm about to share with you. Here it is.

Once the fire gets too big, it's nearly impossible to extinguish it with traditional means. That's when they turn to other tactics, such as stopping the fire's spread, and directing it away from inhabited areas until it burns out. So, what would make this fire spread like oxygen does? The answer came to me immediately. People! People are what causes the fire of the gospel to spread. People who come into contact with God's spirit (which is the heat), and God's word (which is the fuel), can fan the flame into a roaring fire (which is the oxygen)!

So, I started searching my memory for examples of this and I kept coming to the same conclusion. Any time that the spirit of God, and God's Word, come into contact with people whose hearts are open, just like dry wood, they will be lit up. It's a guarantee. It's not something we make, or force. It's just like fire. When the three elements are combined, we have ignition. Once I saw this, I wondered why I hadn't seen it before. Now the trick was to figure out how to keep the fire going, and the key to that was going to be, pouring on the fuel!

I mentioned gasoline engines before, and I apologize if you're not a car person, but it's the easiest analogy to make.

For any red-blooded American teen, one of the rites of passage for about a hundred years, has been learning to drive. Along with operating that huge piece of deadly heavy machinery came at least some basic mechanical knowledge, whether we realized we were learning it or not. I can remember as a teen that my life-blood to be able to go and do and be independent was buying the fuel! Had to get the gas tank filled up, right?

So, I started to think about this analogy as it relates to being a Christian, and immediately, three things came to mind. The first thing was what Paul told us about faith in Roman 10 — it comes by hearing. Next, was Jesus describing faith as a seed.(Matthew 17:20) Finally, I thought about James' statement that faith, without works, is dead. (James 2:26)

These three things paint a clear picture of how we have to fuel our life with God if we want to get lit and stay lit, and with any hope of spreading it. It's more than just evangelism by osmosis. We can't hope to share the story by just absorbing it and hoping others absorb it from us. It requires intentional effort on our part and the Bible is pretty clear as to what that looks like. To give you a closer look I'm going to dive into these three topics. Ready?

First, a lesson from the Apostle Paul, about how people come to know about Jesus.

It's in the book of Romans, chapter 10. Paul is discussing Moses, and talking about how God gave his law to the Hebrews so they would know who He was and what kind of a God He would be to them. But even though they had the law and the prophets, which as Paul explains, pointed straight toward the messiah, not all of them had followed Jesus. All that was necessary was for them to confess with their mouths the truth of Jesus. But until they had that information, what was there to confess? The problem was, no one had told them. They hadn't heard!

For whatever reason, God had hidden His Savior in a bit of a mystery, and not all of the Hebrew teachers and Rabbis had picked up on it. In fact, a huge portion of the Hebrew population was still waiting for the Messiah to come.

Partly because they hadn't heard about Jesus, partly because they were waiting for a political leader to set them free from the Roman Empire. Even though Jesus fulfilled every prophecy they'd been taught to watch for their whole lives, something wasn't clicking.

Think of it like this. All of your friends are talking about the latest movie they want to see.

They've all seen the trailer and they're super excited about going. But not you. You didn't see the trailer. It's not that you don't believe your friends, but something's missing in your understanding. You didn't experience that moving film clip, hear the amazing soundtrack, see your favorite actors twenty feet high on that screen doing amazing things. You didn't hear about it in a way that really grabbed your attention! So, you're not that excited. Maybe if someone showed it to you, but no one has.

That's what it's like for people who don't know about the Gospel. We're running around telling them how exciting it all is. We're pumped about Jesus, but they've only heard us describe our experience of seeing the trailer. They haven't actually seen it for themselves, so they have no real faith to go on. That sense of wonder we've experienced isn't translating, because we're not sharing the whole story! A lot of times, because we don't know it well enough, and that's a problem too.

Paul finally determines what the problem is. He says, "People come to faith in God, because someone preaches the good news about Jesus to them," or "Faith comes by hearing the Word of God." Then he keeps going. He asks a basic question, which is this, "How can anyone ever hear the good news, if no one is sharing it with them?"

The answer is, they can't. That's not just bad news for them, it's bad news for you too. Here's why.

A fire requires constant feeding—the heat has to stay high and the fuel has to stay plentiful for the fire to grow bigger. As it gets bigger the more oxygen it needs to consume. You as a believer require that feedback loop of others sharing their experiences with you, and you sharing yours with them. Not just one time, but over and over in community until it becomes our way of life. No fire ever reached its potential isolated from more heat, fuel, and oxygen.

We need that sharing experience. It's important, and we're going to talk about it more in Section 3 of this book. But let me take a minute to just say: if no one had ever shared that with you, would you even be reading this right now? You wouldn't, and here's why.

You wouldn't have any fire to begin with, nothing to keep lit. So, you could be stopping the expansion of God's Kingdom by not sharing, and preventing your own fire from continuing to burn bright. Think about it.

———— *Chapter Nine* ————

PLANTING YOUR FAITH

The second thing that occurred to me about the fire triangle and the life of a Christian was something Jesus shared with his disciples about faith and seeds and I think it's a much bigger deal than most Christians make it. In fact, I think it reshapes the idea of faith into something powerful and lifegiving, rather than a "grit your teeth and hang on" mentality that requires you jumping through mental hoops to maintain enough "belief" to keep going.

Sometimes, we get all wrapped up in the idea that faith is just "believing." Wow, that would be nice. Wouldn't it? So, if we just never stopped believing, we'd have all the faith needed to heal the sick, give sight to the blind, move mountains, and raise the dead like Jesus promised. We could end world hunger by just multiplying the food, empty the hospitals, stop all the wars, and all live in one big happy family. Well, it might be a little more complicated than that.

Great, Kelly, you're going to tell a story, aren't you?

Follow me real quick and I'll explain. I'm going to go into detail about the event, because I want you to see something. In fact, if you don't get anything else from this book, I want you to pay close attention right here.

This is how you're going to build a relationship with God that is not only sustainable, but will sustain you through every storm that life throws at you. Remember that this is Jesus' example of what faith looks like. Ready? You can find the story in Matthew 17

As Jesus and his disciples were traveling the countryside spreading the good news and they found this dude who was suffering. His son was sick. Demon possessed. He had seizures so bad he'd sometimes fall into the fire and burn himself, and had also fallen into the water. The man was afraid his son would burn to death or drown. He had tried everything, but nothing seemed to help.

Then we find out something interesting. The disciples had already met and dealt with this guy. In fact, they had tried to treat his son, but with no results. They had tried to heal him of his condition, and yet the boy remained exactly the same. To me, it's kind of amazing, since he'd already asked Jesus' followers for help, that he sought Jesus out at all. I mean, a lot of people these days look at Christians they know and want nothing to do with God. I know you've heard that story, and when I meet some of those believers, I can't blame them. Jesus and Christianity get a bad rap from some of our behavior. But this guy knew that Jesus could help.

We're told in other stories about how the crowds would push in around Jesus. I kind of imagine that getting close enough to catch his attention was something like getting the autograph of your favorite musician. Everyone wanted a piece of him, but this guy makes his way through it and begs Jesus to help him So, Jesus tells this stressed out dad, please bring your son to me.

Picture it, the crowd is watching, Jesus raises his hands for silence, the disciples are sure to be nervous, because they couldn't do it. Some of them were just cocky enough they probably figured there was no cure for this kid's epilepsy and mental madness. I'm guessing it was pretty tense.

Now, in other cases, Jesus engaged in a bit of theater. He'd spit in people's eyes, or spit in the dirt and make mud and rub it on them. Or he'd command them to get up and walk. One woman touched Him was healed, and Jesus felt power leave his body. But here, we're not given any big description of the events that followed after the man brought his son to Jesus. It just says that he healed him.

His seizures are just gone and he was restored to his senses instantly.

When I think about why Jesus did it this way there are a million scenarios that come to mind, but I think one of the most likely was this. That father and son had been through enough. If you've ever seen anyone have a seizure, it's traumatic. It can even be embarrassing to them. They lose control. And I'm guessing Jesus wanted to quietly restore this family's dignity, rather than make a big deal out of it.

In fact, he's not even recorded as using them as an object lesson as he often did. He doesn't say a word about them, and they're not mentioned again. They quietly go back to their everyday lives. That, I think, was Jesus' plan for this young man all along. We probably wouldn't hear anything else about it if the disciples didn't bring it up. They take him aside, understandably embarrassed. The conversation could have gone a little like this.

"Uh, sorry we could have handled that for you, but we tried. So, why couldn't we heal him?"

"Yeah, was it in the words you were praying? Because I'm pretty sure John laid hands on him in the same way. It's just weird. It didn't work."

Jesus sighs.

"No, really, we did it just like you showed us…"

He puts a finger on Peter's lips to shush him.

He says one word, "Faith."

Stunned silence for a minute, then a protest.

"Faith? What about faith? I mean, I've got faith, and I know I can speak for the rest of us. We've all got plenty of faith…"

"Do you?" Jesus says. (My version of Jesus is often just a little sarcastic.) "Do you really though? Look, I'm just telling you, if your faith was even like a mustard seed, you could plant that in your soul and say to that mountain over there, rip yourself up from the ground and go jump in the ocean, and that mountain would have no choice but to obey you!"

I imagine Jesus taking a breath and letting it out slow, "I only want to say this once, okay? When you really understand faith and have it, I mean, really have it. Nothing will be impossible for you."

Whoa! Did you hear that? So, we know that faith comes by hearing, and it's like a seed, but what do you do with a seed? Well, I think I've already mentioned this, but before a seed can become anything, it has to be planted. So, let's go back and talk about how our faith gets planted. Ready? Because once you get this, I mean, really get this, nothing in God's kingdom will be impossible for you.

Faith is much more than belief. Belief is giving mental assent to the truth of something. That's good, but it's not enough. This faith thing is like a seed of belief that's planted in the soul and grows into something much more solid. The writer of the book of Hebrews says it this way in chapter 11.

Now faith is the substance of things hoped for, the evidence of things not seen.

Does that sound like mere "believing" to you? I think it's a lot more than that. It starts as belief, just like an apple seed starts as a tiny black kernel. But it grows into something more, just like an apple tree that produces more apples.

And those apples have seeds that produce more trees, until an entire orchard can come from a single seed. That's more than just believing, isn't it?

Here's what I think happens. The Bible also tells us in Romans 12, Paul is talking about giving yourself up as a living sacrifice. We talk a lot about this part, but down in verse three is a concept that doesn't get much air time. Paul says that every person gets a measure of faith from God.

I want to say that again, because I think it's so cool. To every person ever created, God gives a kernel, a seed, a measure of faith. Even in our ability to believe, it starts with Him first giving us that ability, but that's not all!

Paul was the same one who said that faith was packed with evidence of the things we haven't seen yet. Although I rarely use this word, I love how the King James says it's the substance of things hoped for. That word substance means "concrete ingredients." In other words, that tiny mustard seed of faith—just like an actual seed—contains the blueprint and the necessary ingredients to build it into what you're believing for.

Faith in God, then, contains the blueprint and starter ingredients for a wonderful walk with God. We have faith for so many things, what if all of them are seeds of dreams from God? Wouldn't that be amazing? What we know for sure is that Bible says faith in God works this way.

Planting this faith then, is, in and of itself an act of belief, just like planting the apple seed we talked about earlier. You put that little kernel in the ground, and you water it and hope. It goes down into the ground and dies as a seed, splitting itself open, to produce a shoot that given enough time, sunlight, water, and nutrients, will produce millions more seeds in the apples it will provide.

To me, this is how faith works. It's way more than believing.

So, when we start this fire with God, we've got what we need to get it going, and it's up to us to add the sunlight, nutrients and water. It's up to us to make sure the weeds don't strangle it. We have to keep the fire burning. Talk about a mixed metaphor, as long as you don't try to burn your tree, you'll be all right.

——————— *Chapter Ten* ———————

$100 BILL PRINTING BIBLE

So, now I had to fit these ideas into my triangle. I didn't want to jam it in there, but if all of this was true, there had to be a way to make this work.

I'd already discovered that I thought the second leg of the triangle (fuel) was getting filled up with Godly fuel. But you could only attend so much church, read so much Bible, listen to so many albums and podcasts. There had to be something more to the equation and I knew it had to do with planting this seed!

So, what did this mean for my fire triangle? My first model was this—get filled up. This is something we hear all the time. If you don't go to church, get into the word, listen to people talk about God, it's hard to stay focused, hard to make an impact in your own life, forget anyone else's. I felt pretty good about that. But somehow it was still lacking a critical element.

Then I thought, wait a minute. There are a lot of people who never even get that far! Sure, they got the spark, even had enough fuel to fan a small flame. In other words, they said, "Hey, I want to follow Jesus. That sounds good." Then they might have said a few things about committing to it, but then that was it. Poof! The fire died almost immediately. Why?

Well, they had no more fuel.

The few dried twigs of enthusiasm that got them up to the altar, weren't enough to keep them burning the next Monday at home, in school, or at the office. They needed to learn about God, the ways of God, and what it actually means to be a disciple, but they didn't take the time to actually do it. They never planted and nourished that seed into anything more.

They're a lot like some people Jesus talks about in Matthew 25.

He said, the Kingdom of heaven is kind of like ten women, invited to an amazing wedding. They were so excited to go, but since it was night, they needed lamps for light. So, they grabbed their lamps and headed out to meet the groom. Not all of these girls were the same though. Half of them thought ahead and added extra oil, in case it took longer for the groom to meet them and let them in to the wedding feast, while the others followed without filling their lamps!

So, when the groom was late, the five girls without oil fell asleep and left their lamps burning. You can guess what happened. When they woke up, they found they were out of oil. They looked around and realized that the other five girls had plenty. So, they asked them to share, but they can't. The five girls whose lamps were going out realized they had to do something. The wedding party was going down soon and they would literally be "in the dark." They ran to the nearest store to buy oil and when they came back, it was too late. The venue was full and the groom was unable to let them in. They missed out on the party.

Sometimes this story gets interpreted as being about heaven and hell. That could very well be, but I think it also applies to our everyday Christian life. Those who are ready get used by God. They get to do the cool stuff, like loving on people and helping to build the kingdom. Those who aren't ready, end up sitting by themselves in the dark. Better luck next time.

So, what is it Christians don't get about fueling up? To some it just doesn't seem important.

You invite them to worship and they're always working, or playing, or just too tired. But I bet if they heard that the preacher was going to share the secret to becoming a billionaire and anyone who was there was going to get a kit that was guaranteed to make them one in five years—and it had never failed—they would definitely show up.

They may truly want to make a difference in the world, but they're never there to hear the word, and their Bibles sit on a shelf collecting dust. I wish I could create a Bible that printed $100 bills for every page a person read and took to heart. Maybe then my job would be easier.

The good news is, there are enough of us that are listening to Him and to the Word, to make a difference. In fact, all God really needs is one person to make a huge difference. If you don't believe me, pick up your Bible and read it. Or get my first book Reckless Love Revolution and check out some stories about how one person with the love of God and a seed of faith, can change things in a big way! We are getting fueled up.

As I thought about this I noticed, even for the people who realized the value of getting into the things of God, circumstances still weren't changing very fast. Or, they'd make a little progress, get that flame glowing, then let it die down. They were doing that old one step forward, two steps back shuffle. Some of them had been doing it for years! Not only that, but they were teaching others that this was the Christian life. So, new believers were getting mentored in the ways of being a lukewarm Christian right out of the gate!

Then, I realized that getting the fuel wasn't enough either. There were plenty of people who'd been exposed to the source of ignition—God and his spirit—that were in church every time the door was open and never turned their radios off K-Love! Plus, they were almost obnoxious with how much Bible they quoted about everything there was! But, some of them were still flickering out. Something was missing from the equation. Everything I'd tried to make the formula work was coming up short.

That's when I thought back to my childhood summers in Oklahoma mowing the lawn. If you've ever worked with a lawnmower more than a little, you know. It requires spark, fuel, and air to start and stay running. And if you've ever pulled a cord, over and over, without it starting, only to realize, you're out of gas, you know what I'm about to say!

While hiking with that gas can down to the Seven Eleven and putting a couple of bucks worth of gas in it will get you fuel. However, it will not, under any circumstances, start that mower, until and unless you take the final action to make that fuel usable! You've got to put it in the tank! Otherwise, you'll break your arm pulling that rope and the grass will just keep on getting taller. Without pouring it into the tank, the gasoline is completely useless to the lawnmower. In the same way, until we take action on what we hear and think about, all the good "Jesus-y" thoughts in the whole Kingdom of Heaven won't help us stay lit!

Until we take action on what the Word of God says to us, that fuel might as well be in that gas can, or back at the Seven Eleven six blocks away from your lawn mower!

So, how do we do it? What kind of action can we take? It absolutely, positively, with one-hundred-percent certainty, must start with little old me. The person staring back at you in the mirror. Until you put that fuel onto the fire of your life, until you let the Word of God impact you personally, it will do no one else any good.

In James Chapter 2, the brother of Jesus tells us this, I'm paraphrasing.

Who cares if people say they have faith? What does it matter unless they act on it? Can that inactive faith do anyone any good? If someone in their neighborhood needs clothes, will that kind of faith magically clothe them? What if they're hungry, can that faith without any action feed them?

You might say, "Well, I'll just tell them to go to in the peace of God" but if you don't share food or clothes with them, has your faith done anyone any good? No! It's dead! It needs action to be activated!

I know what you're going to say, "Well, you have fancy actions, but I have faith!"

Fine! Show me how your faith helps anyone without action, and I'll show you how my faith works through my actions.

It's cool that you believe in one true God, but man, even the Devil does that and it makes him afraid. But listen, faith, unless you take action on it, is dead.

James was pretty fired up about that. I love it. I love how he turns it around on us and says, basically, prove it! Prove that you have faith. The only way to prove that you really believe, that you really follow the teachings of Jesus, is of course, to act on them. Am I right?

Since faith comes through hearing God's Word, you're taking the first step. That's good. It's better than good. It's great. But you need it to "renew your mind." You need it to change you from the inside out. You ultimately need to let it inspire you to begin changing your world with the actions you take, based on what you learned.

You need to be turning that seed into a tree like the tree David talks about in Psalm 1. We'll talk more about that in a minute.

Let me put it this way. If your parents told you that they loved you every day, multiple times a day, but every time they sat down for dinner, they told you to go buy your own food, earn your own way, find your own place to sleep, find your own ride to school, would you believe their profession of love? If they had it in their power to meet those needs, wouldn't you expect them to act on that love and provide for you? Loving people with the heart of God is no different.

Now If you're thirty and able bodied, I'm not talking to you. You need to get a job. However, if your mom will feed you past thirty and she's okay with it, more power to you. Now, where was I?

Getting lit is amazing. It's a good first step. However, if your spark immediately sputters out every time you get a little glow going, that's a problem. It reminds me of a guy the Bible talked about in the first chapter of James. James was telling his audience that they needed to both hear God's Word, and act on it. He said if they didn't, they were lying to themselves when they claimed to believe in it. Then he told a little parable of sorts.

See, there was this guy, who was really concerned with his appearance, so he dressed himself up and claimed to be well dressed. He stepped up to the mirror and admired his reflection. Then he stepped away from the mirror, but almost immediately he forgot what he looked like. All day long he kept running back to the mirror to remind himself of how well dressed he is.

That's what it's like if you hear God's word, but you refuse to let it change you, and you further refuse to take action to help others with the Word you've heard. You hear it and you think, Oh yeah, that's who I want to be. You might even spend a lot of time thinking about it and making yourself feel good about it, but nothing changes inside. Then, you leave church, you turn off your positive music, and you forget who you said you were a minute ago. Nothing has changed! Know anybody like that?

It's like you've got that $100-bill-printing Bible, but then you just walk out into the street and start dropping it on the ground for the wind to blow away! It's not sticking! Why?

I think Psalm chapter 1 paints about the clearest picture of what a real believer looks like. Solomon calls him the "Righteous Man." Check out what he says about him. I'm paraphrasing here, because I think it's important that we all see ourselves in this.

How blessed are those

That do not go to wicked people for advice

Or walk with those who are guilty of abusing others

Or spend time with those who do nothing but mock others

They find joy in the principles of God

They think about God's way of doing things all day every day

They are like trees planted near clear, moving water

They yield fruit when it's time, every time

Their leaves don't turn brown and fall off

They are successful in everything they do

That's not how the wicked are

They are like dried grass in the wind

That's why they don't stand up to God's examination

And abusive people can't find community with the righteous

God guards the path of the righteous

But the path that leads to wickedness and abuse will be destroyed

Obviously, Solomon is not talking about an actual tree. He mentions them walking and talking, taking action and sharing about it with others. He shows us clearly what he's observed about people who do the right thing, who get on fire for God and stay on fire for God. It benefits them in ways they don't even intend. It affects every area of their lives. This is another of those places though, where the Bible repeats a theme. Solomon, I think, understood something about faith as a seed.

But what does it say about those who don't know, or forget who they are? It's very similar to what Jesus said about the five women who forgot to bring extra oil, isn't it? They are shut out. Not because we judge them; they simply don't fit with those who want to do things God's way. It's not a good fit. In fact, Solomon said, God is going to erase their abusive ways.

To me, this is a picture of someone who not only knows who God is (heat), but understands what He's about and how He expects us to treat others (fuel), and shares it with others (oxygen). That's how you get to be a healthy tree. I'm sure that's what you've always wanted. To be a big oak, or maybe a pine? I'm joking. But the community thing sounds good. Having your work blessed sounds good too, right? But mostly, it's about peace and being established in life to where you know who you are and what you're about.

——— *Chapter Eleven* ———

THE FIRE WAS COMING

Living up to our full potential is really what this book is about. It's not about the attendance numbers on Sundays, or how many people came forward during your last revival. It's about something bigger than a religious institution. I hope you get that. It's about Kingdom. A better word for us today might be "community."

Kingdom gives me a feeling of conquering something, of taking over. But we're invited, all of us, to participate in this Kingdom; and the word community is from the same root as "communion." For example, the Lord's Supper. It's about give and take--something that's both sustained by us, and it sustains us. To me that's much more powerful than any empire built on force. That's what Jesus described, and ultimately, that's why it matters if we get lit, stay lit and spread it. That's what we're living for. That's what will bring glory to God.

That's why I feel like this message is so important, and why it mattered to me to figure out the third leg of this analogy. It just wouldn't let me go. Once I realized that other people provided the oxygen to feed my own fire, I noticed how that worked out in my own life. When I came back to Jesus and dedicated my life to ministry, my entire aim has been to be a light in the world. But as I paid attention to my own fire, I noticed something odd.

It didn't seem like I was burning very brightly. At all.

It was like when you take your phone out in the sunlight. You're squinting to see the screen, but you can barely make out whether your phone is on at all — until you shade it. That same phone screen light, though, will save your life in the Lego minefield of your living room while you're trying to make it to the kitchen in the dark for a glass of water. I felt that I was more like that phone in direct sunlight.

In fact, there were times as I looked back through the last few years of attending Bible college, starting a traveling ministry, that I could barely even see my own light. It did not stand out from the world around me. At first, I got down about that. I thought, "God, if my light isn't bright now, with all of the energy I'm putting into this, will it ever be enough?" I thought about this for a while and couldn't really get an answer until one day Jaxx, my youngest son, came into the garage to "help" me get organized.

If you have kids you already know that when they say they want to help you, what they really mean is this: "Hey dad. I know you're busy, but I want your attention, so let me come and distract you, er, I mean, help you with what you're doing."

Sometimes as a parent, it's easier to just say, "No Buddy. Why don't you spend a little extra screen time?" Sad but true. We distract them from getting in our way when all they really want is to be close to us. I wonder if that's ever how God feels about us? I'm sure it is.

On this day, I got it. I saw my son growing up right in front of me, and I knew I didn't have much time to make that connection.

"Sure Jaxx boy, you can help me," I told him.

Now my mind was running full speed, trying to find something I could give him to keep him busy, where he could talk to me, and I could still get things done.

Fortunately, I didn't need to worry about it. He found something.

"Dad, what's this?"

"It's a flashlight buddy, you know what that is," I replied.

"Cool. Can I play with it?"

This was perfect. I thought back to my own childhood. I'm pretty sure I "played" with my dad's flashlights until the batteries wore out. In fact, I'm pretty sure I remember him being frustrated about it. So, I figured I had a half hour of him contentedly playing with the light. I'd have to recharge it, but I'd get my work done. I turned on the light and handed it to him.

He grabbed it happily and I went to work. It lasted about five seconds. First, he slapped the light. Next, he banged it on his head, then the wall, if I didn't intervene, he was going to break it.

"Whoa, Jaxx, what are you doing? You're going to break it."

"It's not working," he said, shining it in my eyes. It was working just fine. I had to squint to get my sight back.

"Jaxx, it's working fine, look," I showed him the beam.

"Why can't I see it?"

I thought about that one for a second. Then it occurred to me, my garage was too lit up. The little beam of light, which would be a life saver at night in the woods, wasn't making much difference at all.

I could barely make out where it was shining. That's when it hit me. I was like that flashlight.

My job was easy. Staying lit was not that much of a challenge to me. I was surrounded by people trying to be a light. So, I didn't really stand out. Although my preaching had an impact, I realized that if I were to go back into the clubs where I was once an insult comic, my behavior would stand out. Just like that flashlight.

Even though I know that a lot of the fire I see around me turns out to be "strange fire" (like we talked about in section one), the brightness is still there. That's the thing about counterfeits. When it's all mixed in with the real thing, it's hard to pick it out sometimes. The pockets of darkness where those fake fires were burning weren't enough, or maybe my awareness was just not tuned to it. Whatever it was, I wanted to know that my fire was lit.

I needed the contrast of people who didn't know about the light to see it in myself. I wasn't getting enough "oxygen" just standing around in church board meetings and backstage with other traveling evangelists and worship leaders. I needed interaction with people who needed the light to get that oxygen really flowing.

There is something powerful about working to improve yourself, when it comes to connecting with God. When we are in that self-improvement mode; whether mentally, as in getting an education; or physically, as in focusing on what we put into our bodies; or working out, God tends to show up. I think He's showing up all the time, but my brain just has this big blinking, "Open for inspiration," sign on when I'm in that place. Anybody else like that?

For me, it happens a lot at the gym. Sometimes I'm on the treadmill and I just get inspired. I've sent voice messages to my writing partner, out of breath and thumping along on the treadmill, because I didn't want to forget. I just get inspired in the gym.

That's one of the reasons I really like to spend time exercising. Looking at me, you might not realize it, but I'm actually in a lot better shape than I was not that many months ago, and I'm making progress. But, the spiritual workout of having your mind free while your body continues with tasks that don't require the mind's full attention, is amazing.

My morning habit has been hitting the gym. When I'm done with that, I take laps around the gym for two miles, while I pray and meditate on things. So, one morning, while I'm working through this oxygen stuff, God interrupts me.

"Kelly, get in your truck and drive to the country," He says.

Me: "No, I'm good, I'm praying here, let's connect."

Him: "Drive to the country."

It's not that I didn't want to obey God. Although it always costs me something, I find that I have the best adventures when I listen and obey. It's just that I hate the country. I hate it. There's no Wi-Fi in the country. There's no air conditioning in the country. The country sucks. It's hot. There're bugs there. There're no cold drinks there. I just didn't want to go. Finally, I stopped whining, pulled on my big boy pants and got in my truck. Yes, as I'm writing this, I recognize the irony of driving my truck to the country, which I hate.

In the process of founding Reckless Love Revolution I learned a few things about obedience. It so often is not about me. It's not. It's tempting to think that every time God asks you to do something you don't want to do, it's just a test. He's deciding if you're worthy or not. Nope. First, how much more worthy do you need to be? While you were still in rebellion to Him, He sent His son to die for you. I don't see how we can be any more worthy than that.

I've found that there is almost always a practical "why" for what God is wanting me to do.

Sometimes I don't know what it is until later, but many times I find the need I'm supposed to meet. Someone else's blessing is waiting on the other side of my obedience and it's always awesome. Then sometimes you feel like God is just sending you on a wild goose chase, just to see if you'll do it.

So, I left the confines of town, cold drinks, and air conditioning , and although I was clearly well within anyone's definition of "the country" I still hadn't seen a sign of what God wanted from me. Just rows of fences and streets without curbs.

"Okay God, I don't see anyone"

"Keep driving."

I felt like I'd already driven halfway to Kansas, but I rolled on. There was nothing out here. Barns, the occasional horse or cow, rusted mailboxes, abandoned farms, grass, lots of grass. A creek, some trees, the sun, always the sun. Then I saw them. Right there, on the side of the road was a car. I checked my mirrors—no one around for miles. But there they were, parked there with the doors standing wide open.

And I'm thinking, It can't be that easy. It's never that easy.

If you've read my other stories, I always have to ask some awkward question of a total stranger to get to the "meeting the blessing" part. Always. So, I rolled on past. At the next intersection, I realize I'm being silly and I whip it around to go back. But I'm going to qualify this. They're probably just out here smoking a joint and don't care what I'm doing.

"You good?" I ask out my window, prepared to hit the gas back for town.

"Nope, out of gas and we don't have a phone," the driver tells me.

We talk for a minute. I tell them I'm going to help them out, sit tight, I'll be back with some gas. I drive into town, fill a can with gas and head back out. By now I'm getting excited because I just know that the Holy Spirit has gone before me and prepared their hearts. I'm getting ready to either meet some really cool people who are already on fire for Jesus, or they are about to get that way, because that's how I roll! Right?

But, if you know me at all, you've heard me say over and over again that God is not tied to my agenda. My expectations have no bearing on what He will or will not do, other than if I expect Him to show up, He will. Past that, all bets are off.

I mean, we're talking about a God who has shown up in a burning bush, used a whale to transport an evangelist to a preaching gig, talked through a donkey, sent fire from heaven, raised dead people with a prophet's skeleton, and parted an entire inland sea down to dry land for the Hebrews to get away from Pharaoh. To say that the Spirit of God is unpredictable would be an understatement of epic proportions.

On my way back, I'm getting so charged up. I'm thinking through my speech. I know just what I'm going to say and I'm so glad that I didn't turn around and head back too soon. These stranded souls are going to be so grateful to be rescued that they won't know what hit them. Yay God. You and me are a team today. We're getting it done.

Finally, I see the car and roll up beside them. I take the can and put the gas in their car. They're very appreciative. So, I put my can away and right there on the side of the road, I make my move. It's obvious to me that God sent me out here to preach to these poor lost souls today, but just to be safe, I make sure to give them the benefit of the doubt.

"Hey, I don't know if you guys love Jesus or what. But I just wanted to let you know that I was at the gym working out when God spoke to me about your situation. He told me to drive out here, and when I found you, I knew I was supposed to help. To me, that says a lot about how much God loves you, you know? He loves you so much He died for you, and today, in particular, He saw your need and He sent someone to rescue you."

I looked at them expecting to see tears. Or big smiles, at least. Stone cold silence. They nodded in appreciation, but were not moved by my speech in the least. I didn't get it. I didn't understand. Why hadn't it worked?

God had teed this one up for me so perfectly. I should have hit it out of the park. In fact, I was so wrapped up in my part of it, I almost allowed myself to get upset. But, by then, I was starting to understand how oxygen works. The more people that came into contact with this flame, the brighter it would burn. I offered to pray for them and they accepted. I said a few words of blessing and they drove away. Not a single spark or hint of smoke.

But I've been around God long enough to know that things are not always as they appear to be. This wasn't over yet. I knew that God had spoken to me. I had proof. The empty gas can in my truck was enough to convince me of that. It was no coincidence God sent me down this road, on this morning, ready to help whomever I found. This was a long way from over. Just because there was no visible flame—I knew the fire was coming.

———— *Chapter Twelve* ————

FORGET EVERYTHING AND REST

Although I hate camping—because it's in the country—I've been camping enough to know one thing. Embers create fires. As a kid I can remember being told that if you don't completely extinguish the embers of a campfire, they can restart that fire. In fact, they can lay glowing for days, until the wind picks up and a spark spreads to create a wildfire. Like so many things in nature, just because a fire appears dormant don't assume it's over. I'd just loaded those folks on that road with coals, and I just knew something was going to come out of that.

What do you do to get embers to catch fire? You blow on them, and the best way I knew to do that was simple. I did what any 21st-century evangelist would do. I pulled out my smartphone. Right there on the side of the road, with their car fading into the distance, I opened up the camera and started sharing the story. I told how God had spoken to me, about finding them on the side of the road, about going into town for gas and about their response.

I told my audience to be praying, and I shared with them how things like that are not mistakes. I told them how God was going to use this event to spark fire in someone's life. I just knew it. For whatever reason, although I could feel the Holy Spirit burning bright inside of me in that moment, they hadn't caught fire just yet.

Heat wasn't the problem because I was more than hot enough that day. Oxygen was plentiful. They'd been right here with me, but whether their fuel was wet, or just burned up, I didn't know. All I knew was that their kindling didn't spark. Not in that place and time anyway.

The video story went viral on Facebook Live. Something like fifty thousand viewers picked it up, watched it, shared it, and commented on it. It got a lot of traction. I'll probably never know how many fires it started, or boosted. I'll probably never have any idea of how many lives were impacted because of that one story on that one day, as those viewers reached out to impact others, encouraged by what God had done through my obedience that day.

There was no way I could have known what would happen next. In fact, if I were writing this little saga, they'd have somehow seen my video and gotten saved. But that would be way too simple for God. He likes to flex a bit when he weaves a plot, and this one turned out to be pretty epic. Here, before I tell you, just in your own imagination, dream up an ending for this story and let's see if it matches up with the real thing, ready? I can tell already that you're thinking too small. Check this out!

Shortly after that Facebook Live video went viral, among all of the messages I received thanking me and asking for prayer, one stood out. It was from a woman and her message included a photo of a dude. It took me a second to go back through my mental rolodex of faces, and at first I couldn't place him, so I read the message.

"Is this the guy who was driving the car you brought gas to that day? I was watching your video and I think this is him. If it is, you're not going to believe this, but he's my brother."

I got a cold chill down my spine as I looked at the picture again and recognized the driver from the car.

My mind went back to that country road, the sun beating down, both doors open and this guy's face. I kept reading. The message went on.

She explained that she was this guy's sister. He was living life on his own terms and she and some others were very concerned for how it was going to turn out for him. I could hear the love coming through that message. We should all have a sister that cared that much. I got excited all over again as I looked at that picture. I looked back at the message because there was more.

She wrote: "I want you to know that my brother is lost. We started over three years praying for him, and we've waited all this time for an answer. Our prayer was that God would put people in his path to tell him about Jesus. So, when I saw your video and heard he'd run out of gas, I just knew that God was answering our prayers."

Not too long after that, I was on tour with my first book, Reckless Love Revolution. This wonderful woman came three hours out of her way just to meet me. There is nothing more humbling than to have someone come that far just to shake your hand and hear you speak. I was overwhelmed. Not only did she come but she brought two friends who hadn't met Jesus. Now the fire was starting to spread as they got lit!

But the story doesn't end there.

When the embers of God get buried, they burrow deep and burn hot, and these embers keep coming up and starting new flames. After she went home, she spoke to her husband, who happened to be a pastor, and he called me. I went to their church and preached. The embers were spreading, apparently, because seventeen more people got set on fire for Jesus from that one sermon. So, if you're keeping score, that's 19 people that I know of from that one act of obedience. That's a lot of oxygen getting added to those embers. I have no doubt that more will come to faith because of it. Maybe someday I'll get a picture of what it all meant.

This is why it matters if you get lit, and stay lit. I hope you're understanding this as you read this book. But my heart is not just for those of you reading who already know Jesus. I wish you well, I hope you thrive. I hope your adventures with God are ten times better than mine, but here's the thing. You're already in touch with the Creator. I'm writing this to encourage you to stay lit for all of the guys who are out of gas on the side of the road in your life. This book is about that dude's sister and her two friends, and the 17 other souls now burning brightly in her hometown.

When you think of the impact that 19 people can make on the world, it's staggering. If every one of you reading this book right now were to reach out and help 19 people get lit over the course of your lifetime, it wouldn't take long for us to reach the whole world. Remember, fire is a happening. Wherever and whenever the elements come together, it happens! We're not limited to 19!

That's what gets me so excited. Because I know that out of the many people I've been blessed and privileged to share Jesus with, I know a lot of them are carrying the flame. They are burning brightly, a light for everyone to see. That changes so much. It can't be overstated. I mean, as awesome as a big fireworks display is, it won't comfort you on a cold night in the woods, or cook your dinner. Fireworks simply flare up, and then burn up, way up there in the sky and benefits little. It's not sustaining.

It's that sustaining fire of God in the hearts of true, mature believers that really lights up the world. That's why I was so excited about getting to this section of the book—all of the thoughts, feelings, emotions and memories that it stirs up in me.

But what about those who don't survive it? What about those who seem consumed by it? What do we do at times in our life when it feels like the fire of God is burning, not just in us, but burning on us?

Burnout is a real thing. Even for Christians. We hear the world talk about it. Maybe we've even experienced burnout in some area of life. If you haven't yet, it may be because you're young and haven't reached that stage, or maybe you're just truly fortunate. For the rest of us, it can be a harsh reality.

I know I experienced burnout. My hard-living, hard-drinking, hard-loving, hard-rocking lifestyle eventually put me in a place that I was either going to change or die. I knew it. Instead of getting lit God's way, I burned the candle at both ends the world's way; eventually it caught up with me. I remember that feeling. But I don't think it was that different from what I sometimes see strong believers going through.

In the first part of the book we talked about the difference between "being on fire," and "living like you're on fire." How we have to be careful not to jump into God's work in our own strength. I know what that feels like. I experienced it so deeply when I was young. As a teen, it seemed like I was meeting Jesus and getting saved every Sunday. I wanted so much to be on fire for Jesus, but I was going about it the wrong way.

I'd throw away my porn, burn my music and movies, anything that I felt did not honor Jesus. I'd start over. I'd pray. I'd open my Bible and I'd really read it. I'd crank up the Christian music and I'd flood my soul with anything I could find just to get a little closer to what I thought I was supposed to be in my Christian walk.

My behavior was all born out of fear. I was afraid of God. There are two different ways to be afraid of God. One holds terror, the other holds awe. All I could see was that I wanted so much to be saved. I was afraid I wasn't and I was terrified of what would happen if my life ended. So, I'd start the cycle again and I'd burn out just as quick.

Why? Because, the heat was there, and the oxygen was there, but there was no fuel down in my soul. I hadn't really hidden the Word of God in my heart. I was just going through the motions. Obviously, I meant it, but I wasn't getting past the surface. It would hold up about as long as a pretty girl's makeup at a dance. You know what I mean. The least bit of sweat and they're off to find a mirror and touch it up. That was me. My mask constantly needed to be adjusted.

Finally I came to the point where I got set on fire with God. I truly experienced the deep connection with His spirit and I started to understand that it wasn't about pleasing Him with a list of do's and don'ts. When I got that--then it really stuck. Things changed. I was no longer in terror over what God was going to do to me. I learned the real fear of God. That it consisted of a combination of awe, respect, and a longing that made me want to be in his presence and dread any time that I began to slip away from it. At that point, other things in my life began to lose their appeal.

You've probably heard acronyms for fear such as: False Evidence Appearing Real. Mine are a little different. I have two acronyms for fear.

The terror of God that comes from not knowing Him in a real way is Forget Everything And Run. Because that's the only sane response to being afraid of God's wrath.

For those who are truly connected, lit, staying lit and spreading it, everything changes. That's when the fear of the Lord takes on a new meaning: Forget Everything And Rest.

What happens is that we claim we want intimacy with God, but we don't truly have the fear of the Lord in our lives. We haven't come to that place where we realize, like Paul said, all things are permissible for me, but not all things are profitable. God doesn't kick us out every time we fall into temptation, but we're not drawing closer to Him either. (1 Corinthians 6:12)

Here's an example. I love my wife and I want intimacy with her. Hopefully, all husbands have this is a goal. But if on one hand I'm telling her how precious she is to me, while on the other I'm flirting with other women everywhere we go, right in front of her, I'm not going to get that intimacy. James 4 tells us that God is a jealous lover, and to flirt with the world, or to flirt with and tolerate sin, means we are cheating on Him. If I wouldn't expect my wife to be intimate with me after flirting with other women, why would we expect God to be any different?

Just like us humans, God shares His secrets with His friends. And to be clear, the Bible says over and over, God is a friend to those who fear Him.

It's when we get into that place where anything that draws us away from God loses all its appeal—and seems so completely worthless—that we really can be on fire without burning out. When we are so excited with the fruits of time with Him, and meditating on Him, and acting on His Word that we can't wait to just get into His presence. Then we want to go out and share that experience with as many people as we can. That's when we begin to fully understand what it means to Stay Lit.

Make no mistake, I am not suggesting that I can't experience burnout again. I can. You can. We all can. No one is immune. But we don't have to. Any time we start thinking that any of this is about us, we're putting ourselves at risk. Every time we take credit for the move of God, every time we fail to acknowledge His presence, or worse yet, refuse to even invite Him in, we're dancing with danger.

Chapter Thirteen

"TROUBLER OF ISRAEL"

So, what is burnout? In the Bible, fire serves two main purposes. Everywhere it occurs as a symbol of God, it is there for two reasons. First, it comes to burn out what's impure. Second, it's a refining process, it purifies. In the believer's life, burnout serves a purpose too. It comes to destroy any work that wasn't breathed by God, work that we did for our own glory, and it comes to change our hearts and purify us so that our motives become pure.

Remember in the first section when we talked about the sons of Aaron and the "strange fire" they brought to the altar? It consumed them. It burned up their pridefulness and there was nothing left in them to stand before God. Nothing left to purify. Any believer who thinks that they can live this life without the Holy Spirit, or continue down a path that God has said to abandon, will eventually come to a point of burnout.

The sweet thing about God is this. He doesn't desert you. Even if you rebelled and ended up in burnout. Even if you pretended to serve Him, while serving your own selfish desires, and crashed and burned beyond recovery, He cares. He will restore you if you let him. A great example comes from the Old Testament.

Now, before I tell you about Elijah's burnout, I want to show you where he just came from. He was about to have a literal mountain-top experience with God in a very public way. But it wasn't going to last. Here's what happened.

In 1 Kings Chapter 18 we see a showdown brewing, between Elijah and King Ahab. Ahab was probably the most wicked King in the Bible. And in the New Testament, Jesus said that his Cousin John represented the second coming of Elijah. So there's our cast of characters. King Ahab hated Elijah and called him "the troubler of Israel" because Elijah kept calling him out on his bad behavior.

Finally, they agree to a sort of duel—Elijah versus the prophets of Baal. Now Baal is simply a foreign god whom the King's wife, Jezebel, made popular, which was totally against the law of God. The duel is scheduled to take place on Mt. Carmel and there will be a public audience.

So, Ahab sends out a meet-up invite and all the Hebrews come to Mt. Carmel, along with the King's 450 prophets of Baal. Ahab gets up and says a few words.

"Hey! We've been swaying back and forth between serving God and serving Baal, but that's not sustainable! Elijah pointed out that we need to choose. So, here's the deal. One or the other of them is the real God, and if Yahweh is God, you should serve Him. "

I can kind of imagine the prophets of Baal rattling their swords and booing at this. Ahab holds up his hands.

"Okay, okay, but if Baal turns out to be legit, we should serve him!"

Nobody says a word

Then Elijah stands up, and things get real.

"Look, I'm the only prophet of Yahweh left. Meanwhile, the King has 450 prophets of Baal. So, here's the test I think we should use. Get two bulls. One for the prophets of Baal, one for me. We'll cut them up, put them on a pile of wood on the altar, but not light it. Are you with me so far? From there it's pretty simple. The God who wants his sacrifice, can provide his own fire. I'll call on Yahweh, they can call on Baal, whoever burns the bull, gets to be God in Israel? Are you with me?"

The people agree.

Then Elijah says, "Listen, to make it fair, I'm going to let you guys go first. So, choose your bull, cut it up, and put in on the altar, but don't light the fire. I'm watching you."

So, they do.

Then they shout, "Baal consume this sacrifice!" Nothing happens.

So, they decide maybe a dance will help, so they start leaping about. Then they get into their ritual toolkit and decide maybe cutting themselves with knives and spears will get Baal's attention.

Now Elijah starts to talk smack. Seriously, there are some insult comics who should take notes because this boy can spit fire!

"Look, I think he's asleep! You're not shouting loud enough! I can't hear you! Is he on the toilet? Wait, I know, he's gone on vacation, so maybe he'll be back in a little while."

This goes on all afternoon and into the evening. Elijah just waits until they exhaust themselves. Then he stands up.

"People of Israel, come closer," he tells them. As they watch, he repairs this altar to Yahweh on Mt. Carmel that had been destroyed. He restacks the twelve stones, one for each tribe. They just sit there and watch. He digs a moat around the altar. They keep watching. He chooses his wood and stacks it and butchers his bull and puts it on the altar. By now, it must have been getting dark, but Elijah isn't done yet.

"I need 4 volunteers from the crowd," he says. "Take those giant water jars and fill them up. Then bring them back."

People are starting to ask questions. They'd been in a drought for three years without any rain, and that was a lot of water he was asking for just to prove a point.

"What's he doing?"

"No idea, I think he's crazy."

They bring back the water jars and set them down.

"Nope. Pour it over the sacrifice and the altar," Elijah says.

They do it, then they set the jars down and head back to their seats.

"Not so fast!"

They turn back to him.

"Do it again!"

They do.

"One more time!"

The volunteers fill the jars a third time and pour it over the altar.

By now, everything is wet. The bull is wet, the wood is wet, the stones are wet, the dirt around the stones is wet. In fact, the trench around the altar is filled with water. By now the people are sure Elijah has lost his mind.

Somewhere in the crowd there must have been someone who was there when he raised the dead, or healed the sick, so maybe there were a few old timers who hoped he still had a little bit of his old power left.

Then Elijah waits. If you remember the story about the strange fire, we talked about the rules God had made for worship. Part of that set specific times for sacrifices and Elijah was going to play by the rules. Soon it was time for the evening sacrifice so Elijah walks to the altar.

By now, everyone is riveted on this crazy old man. He's built the altar by himself, slaughtered the bull by himself, dug the trench by himself, then had 12 jars of water poured over the whole mess. They couldn't wait to see what happened next. Elijah stands up and prays.

O LORD, God of Abraham, Isaac, and Israel, let it be known this day that You are God in Israel and that I am Your servant and have done all these things at Your command. Answer me, O LORD! Answer me, so that this people will know that You, the LORD, are God, and that You have turned their hearts back again."

I'm sure you could have heard a pin drop in the silence that followed, but only for a second. From the sky, in a flash, came a roaring flame of fire, white hot and searing to the eyes. It struck the altar, setting the sacrifice ablaze, consuming the wood, burning the rocks, roaring down to the very dust that had been muddy just moments before.

A chant rises from the Israelites. "The Lord, He is God! The Lord, He is God!"

The prophets of Baal were probably wetting themselves, and Elijah, I'm sure, let out a huge sigh of relief before leading the people in the beheading of all 450 prophets of Baal.

Wow. Did you get all of that? Talk about getting LIT! Elijah was on fire. He'd just preached a hugely successful revival, complete with a dramatic fiery finale. I would have felt like I was on top of the world. But Elijah still had Ahab to deal with. That's where the burnout comes in.

See, it's not enough to obey God and see amazing things happen. It's funny but sometimes it's easier to trust God to show up and do something radically crazy than it is to trust him in the little things of life. That's what Elijah was about to find out.

Chapter Fourteen

LOCK, STOCK, AND BARREL

Immediately after the showdown on Mt. Carmel, it starts to rain for the first time in three years. This should have made Elijah feel great about his place in God's plan, but how many times do we have a huge success and immediately begin to doubt ourselves and God? I do.

Of course, there was also the death threat from the Queen.

Ahab had gone home and told Queen Jezebel—a woman who was so evil her name is a synonym for a viciously cruel woman—everything Elijah had done, up to and including the dead prophets. Jezebel got all upset and had her scribe take a letter.

To Elijah: "Heard what you did, and may the gods strike me down if by tomorrow you're not as dead as my prophets!"

Elijah, for his part, read the note and freaked out. He took off running into the wilderness. When he finally ran out of steam—remember this guy had been altar-building and bull-slaying—he just dropped to his knees and begged God.

"Kill me now! I'm no better than my fathers!" Then he passed out and slept.

God then sends an angel to tap this dude on the shoulder to wake him up and feed him. Not just once, but twice. Finally, he gets up and walks to a place called Mt Horeb and hides out in a cave. This is where we get to see his burnout.

Let's recap. Elijah challenges the prophets and wins. He kills the prophets, ticks off the queen, gets fed by an angel and he's now on a mountain in Horeb hiding out in a cave. Oh, and don't forget he brought rain for the first time in three years. But now he's undergoing burnout in a major, major way.

While I know I should feel bad for this guy, (because I know what this feels like) but I can't. It actually makes me feel better. Here's why. You know all those places in the Bible where someone does something unbelievably stupid? Peter chops off an ear, Jonah tries to run away from God, David cheats on his wife, has his best friend killed and then steals his wife… Well okay, maybe not that last one. But the rest of them make me feel like maybe I'm going to be all right. Like I might actually fit in with the rest of God's followers down through the ages.

Elijah is no different; he's about to lose his stuffing. He's unraveling fast! Here he is in the cave on Mt. Horeb and darkness falls. Then, when things can't get any creepier in the dark, on a mountain, in a cave, God starts talking to him. Seriously, you'd think after all the times God tells people in the Bible to not be afraid when he talks to them, He would get it that hearing from Him freaks us humans out a little bit.

So, how do you know that things are about to get real with God? He starts talking about Himself in the third person. You can almost hear him sigh impatiently before he says this.

"Get up, get outside in the presence of the Lord, for the Lord is about to pass by."

Translation: Oh, you think Jezebel is scary? You're about to find out. GET UP!

I've heard God talk like this before, not gonna lie. It's like making your Mom mad. You know it won't end well.

So, Elijah gets up and staggers out of the cave in the dark onto the side of the mountain alone. Remember how I said I hate the country, and camping? Yeah. This is worse. He's clinging to the side of this scrub-brush covered rock, and God sends a windstorm. In fact, the Bible uses language here that I find interesting. Being from Oklahoma, I know about windstorms. It's like He's talking about the Wizard of Oz here. It says there was a great and powerful wind. Not only that, but although I've been around tornadoes my whole Life, I've never seen stones "shattered" by wind. That's a serious, serious storm.

But God's presence isn't in it.

I imagine Elijah looking up to heaven muttering, "Hey God. Are we done yet? Either let me sleep, or kill me."

Next, the mountain starts to shake with a mighty earthquake. Ironically, since fracking, this is something Okies also know about. Elijah is scrambling for handholds now on this shattered mountainside. It's dark, he's alone, he's afraid and now God is trying to shake Him loose, but God's presence is not in the quake.

"What next, God? A giant flood?"

"No, wise guy, I promised I wouldn't do that again, remember?"

"Do I smell smoke?"

The next thing Elijah knows, the mountainside is engulfed in a raging fire. But still, he did not sense God's presence.

This story is starting to sound familiar.

One night, a few years back, in the winter, Oklahoma had a night like this. Our state, I'm pretty sure, became the only place on earth to experience tornadoes, an ice storm, earthquakes, flash flooding, and out-of-control wildfires all in one night.

No, this is not a joke. If that wasn't bad enough, one of the storms hit a tiger sanctuary, and for a hot minute, Central Oklahoma was like the set of Jumanji!

Just as Elijah is bracing himself for the next onslaught, things change. It gets still and there, in the quietness, comes a small whisper. Finally, God was here. He pulled his cloak over him and stood in the mouth of his cave.

"What do you think you're doing here?" God asks His prophet.

I love the language here when Elijah replies.

"I have been very zealous for the Lord God Almighty. Really, I'm going all out, in front of everyone! But your people, the Israelites, are losing it! They've already killed all my prophet buddies with swords, and there was so much blood. I am the only one left, the only one who hasn't worshiped other Gods and now they want me dead too!"

This guy is burned out. Done. Down to an ember. Remember him just a couple of chapters before, swaggering out in front of the people, challenging the king, using up precious water like it was nothing? Taunting all those prophets? Now look at him, whimpering in a cave. He's so afraid he cannot even speak to God directly, just about Him.

He was so sure God had his back that he risked his own life in front of 450 heavily armed prophets of Baal and the same Israelites who killed the other prophets that he was willing to taunt them. He made fun of these guys. Seriously! I mean, he's up there like David Copperfield or something.

"Watch very closely as we soak the sacrifice not once, not twice, but three times. Here from our audience is my culinary expert. What do you say, Jacob? Will it burn?"

"No."

"Once more for the people in the cheap seats. You're saying this is so soaked it's not going to catch on fire, is that right?"

"Yes!"

And although he was so on fire right after that he actually outran the King's chariot back to town after slaughtering the prophet. But now he's huddled in a cave, the man who has such a connection with God he can call down fire from heaven, in a muddy mess of tears, sweat, and fear. Come on Elijah, have some respect for yourself, brother. Except, we all know how he feels, don't we?

But God isn't impressed, and here's an important lesson. When you say, "Here I am, send me." When you put in your application to be on fire for God, you're His. Lock stock and barrel. And while He won't force you to do things, He's also not always going to sit by while we sulk in self-pity and that's how He is with Elijah right now. He's got a plan and Elijah is part of it. He's not going to wait for Elijah to find his Mt. Carmel attitude.

Now, God doesn't say, "Put on your big girl panties and get over it."

(But I'm pretty sure it's in the subtext here.)

"No, you're not the only one, Elijah. There are seven hundred that I saved-- not that it's any of your business. Now get up from there and wipe your face. You look like a mess. Go back the way you came to the desert of Damascus. I've got a new king and we are about to flip the script on Ahab. Not everything is about you, bro."

118

Right here, when God is right in the middle of revealing His plan, when He's just about to save His people from the tyrant Ahab, Elijah (who is the most powerful of all Old Testament prophets), gets all in his feels and burns out. He starts to think that God's plan revolves around him and that he just can't do it anymore. But God sets him straight.

As I close out this section, I want to be very clear about this. Although God calls us and needs us to engage for his Kingdom to come to pass, it's not all about us. Although we are called to build, encourage, and maintain the fire in our souls, that fire is His. He is the power behind the heat, the sustaining force of the fuel, and the mighty wind that brings oxygen when we feel our embers are about to go out.

SECTION THREE - SPREAD IT

Chapter Fifteen

BOTTLE ROCKETS, PART 2

I know I said I hate the country, but it does have its perks. For instance, when you're in the mood to play stupid games with bottle rockets, there's no better place to do it. Unless of course, it's tooling down I-35 in a van at 70 miles an hour.

While the biker-chase scene is definitely in the highlight reel of stories that need to be told at my memorial, it was a one-time event. Most of my other bottle rocket incidents were much less dangerous, or seemed that way to me. However, there was one time that it almost got out of control.

When Jesus said, "Go into all the world and preach the gospel," He was laying out the master plan for how the Kingdom was going to be built. It would be made up of every tribe, color, tongue, and gender. It would be a place where men, women, and children could stand equal before the creator and it would require a wildfire of spreading this news to get it done. He knew that.

He also knew that his closest disciples would be executed. This included Peter who was crucified upside down because he didn't feel worthy to share the same death as Jesus. Jesus knew that the very forces of hell itself would line up to stop the Kingdom from happening, but He had a plan, and it included a raging fire so big it couldn't be stopped. I almost started one of those once.

If you recall my buddy Bob (we're still calling him Bob just in case there're any outstanding warrants), was a willing participant with me in my bottle rocket hijinks. When you're traveling the country trying to live the Rockstar life, you get bored on the open road. When that happens, there's little that can get your blood flowing like running from actual explosives down a country road.

So, this one time—not at band camp—we were in such a mood of boredom and we just happened to have a sack of said rocket fueled projectiles on hand. So, we took the nearest exit and headed off the highway into the dark country night. It didn't take us long to spot the perfect location for our game of Bottle Rocket Chicken. If you don't remember from my first story you basically point one at yourself, light the fuse, and run with it chasing you.

On this particular night, we were just over the north border of Texas from Oklahoma and it was a still summer night. The road we'd picked was gravel and moonlit—a perfect surface for outrunning rockets—with waist-high sawgrass on either side. Had I known then what I know now about the Fire Triangle, I might have pegged that dry, tall grass for what it was: i.e., perfect wildfire kindling. AKA, fuel. But I didn't. Or I just didn't care. Probably a little of both.

So, Bob and I lined up the rockets and we broke out the lighters. We checked the road ahead for obstacles and on the count of three, we lit the fuses and took off. What happened next is a mystery. When I tell this story, some people say I must have gotten some poor-quality rockets. Others say that the gravel was at fault. Whatever. I'm just glad to have survived the incident.

As pounded down this road in the summer night, the high beams of our minivan lighting up the clouds of dust from our footsteps like low-lying smoke, we heard the rockets kick in. I felt one graze right past my ear, and I slowed down as it exploded ahead of me. I looked over at Bob. He was stopped, his eyes wide as the second rocket veered horribly off course and took a dive into the tall grass along one shoulder of the road.

At first, it seemed like everything was fine. The rocket had popped, and there was a bit of smoke, but no serious damage.

"Oops," I said. We both laughed. Too soon.

With a whoosh, it was like the whole shoulder of the road was on fire. We ran back toward the van and tried to stomp it out, but the heat, fuel, and oxygen combo were in the sweet spot and this fire was happening. We stood a few seconds, trying to decide if there was anything we could do. We tried. We really did. We took off our shirts and fiercely beat the ground trying to put the fire out. We ran back to the van to get the half empty soda bottles to pour on the flames. Nothing was working.

This must have taken longer than it felt because we were completely exhausted when we heard a siren in the distance. There were no houses in the immediate vicinity, and with the firetrucks on the way, we figured it would be okay. So, we hopped in the van and booked it toward the highway.

As we drove away, we could see spectators gathering on the side of the road, and the entire field looked like it was on fire. No one was looking at us, so we drove on, passing the firetruck as it bawled its way from pavement onto gravel and floated along in a bright red cloud of dust toward the scene of the crime.

It was pretty quiet in the van that night. Later we caught a newscast, and heard that the fire had been put out, but not before it consumed a huge area of grassland.

It was like one of those moments when your mom's predictions about running with scissors plays out in front of your eyes.

Of course, I knew that fire was dangerous, but until you actually witness it spread, you can't understand the massive potential it carries to affect large areas almost instantaneously.

The one thing I think that struck me was how little heat it actually took to set so much fuel on fire! Up to that point in my life, it had seemed stupid to me that bottle rockets were illegal. In my mind, they were barely more than a glorified flying firecracker, but that whole field was ablaze faster than we could even react. Even if we'd had a fire blanket, it would have been too late. (Remember that. We'll talk more about it later.)

That was the clearest picture I'd ever seen of what a soul on fire for God, spreading His light to the world, could really look like. It drove home that lesson I'd learned when I was ten years old about who shows up when you light a fire. Before we'd even managed to get out of sight, people were stopping to watch it burn and just moments later, the fire fighters were on their way to put it out. Those who want to watch the world burn, and those convinced it is their job to put it out are always on hand when fire is involved.

Life with Christ is no different. As soon as you make that connection and the spark takes off in your own life, people start to show up and almost without fail, they fall into two categories, the curious and the concerned—the ones that want to put your fire out. For most of us in early twenty-first century America, the most we'll endure is some rude comments and the occasional cussing out. Not so for the believers in the New Testament.

In Luke Chapter 21, Jesus and the disciples are in the temple. He's been teaching them about giving and what true generosity looks like, but some of the disciples are distracted by the physical temple and how beautiful it is, so Jesus tells them it's going to all be torn down.

"When is this going to happen?" they asked.

"Oh, you'll know" He told them. He goes on to describe the sacking of Jerusalem that would happen within some of their lifetimes in 70 AD. Then he says this about the people that will show up to put out their fire.

They will arrest and abuse you, they will turn you over to religious authorities, or throw you into jail. You'll be forced to testify before politicians and rulers because of the fire in you. But it's okay, this will give you a chance to share with them. Listen, decide now that you're not going to sweat your own defense, okay? I promise, I'll put just the right thing to say in your heart when the time comes. You'll sound so wise, they won't know what to say. You'll be irresistible.

The worst part though, is that it won't stop there. Your own family will turn on you. They'll even execute some of you. You'll be hated by society if you choose to follow me. Here's the deal. I will protect you so that not a hair on your head can be touched. Have some guts. Stand up and be counted, because the reward is real life.

What? Have you ever read the Bible and get so confused you almost squint? Yeah, look at the end of that. Not a hair will be touched, except for those who are tortured and killed. I think this goes back to what we heard Paul say about how we're not really a part of the physical world anymore. We're in it, but not of it. The Kingdom of God is here and now, but it's also in this in-between place where things are not always what they seem. What Jesus is saying is this. They can't touch your essence. The spirit—the real you, not the flesh body you're driving around in—the real you will not be damaged. It will be delivered whole into the next life no matter what happens here. That's pretty cool.

Even with Jesus' dire predictions, what we're going to talk about next is the easy part of the Get Lit, Stay Lit, Spread it paradigm.

I say that because, just like that bottle rocket fiasco that Bob and I were part of (allegedly), once you get enough fuel, heat, and oxygen in one place, all it takes is a tiny spark to set the whole world on fire.

We know this, because although everything that Jesus prophesied in the Temple that day came true, it stopped nothing. In fact, the more the Empire stomped on the fire that those first-century followers of "The Way" represented, the further those embers scattered!

—— *Chapter Sixteen* ——

"I'M AN EVANGELIST. ARE YOU?"

In my first book, Reckless Love Revolution, we told a few stories about "embers." Individuals who impacted entire cultures for the Kingdom. People like the Ethiopian eunuch who took the gospel to Africa; the woman at the well who spread the fire of the gospel in Samaria; and the Gadarene Demoniac, free from his evil spirits, who spread the word across the surrounding countryside.

So what can stop us? It's simple. Believers who've been lit, but never quite get to the staying and spreading part. Why does this happen? Why are there some people who seem, as Paul said, to have a form of godliness but deny the power that exists in it? (2 Timothy 3:5) It can happen for a couple of reasons.

In Section 2, we talked about burnout and how it can happen to those who get into their own flesh and serve God out of terror of what could happen if they don't. Just like I was as a teen. In that state, the fear of sin and punishment can do a lot to dampen your flame. The guilt and shame of not being able to overcome those urges will prevent you from saying much. Why? Fear of being found out as a fraud.

Remember? Forget Everything And Run!

It's been going on since the garden of Eden when Adam found out he was naked and hid from God. It's a normal human reaction to things we don't understand. It's easy to end up there, and here's a word of caution. If you see someone in that position, don't fall into the temptation of judging that person. That pride that enters in when you get that feeling of superiority will also squash the desire to spread it.

Maybe you've heard this conversation before.

"Why don't you talk to your friends and family about Jesus?"

"Well, they're just not the right kind of people. They're not fit for church."

Pride will have you judging the quality of the "oxygen" before you even light the fuel! That's not good. Jesus never qualified who was good enough for His message. Ever. There were times He couldn't bring the whole package, because their hearts were in the wrong place, but that never meant they weren't good enough to be redeemed. They just weren't ready yet.

Remember those 19 people whose lives were changed when I talked to the guy stranded by the side of the road? He wasn't into it, but they were ready. I could have spent a few minutes talking to them and found that out, and never even mentioned the gospel. But, that time at least, my pride didn't get involved, and then I realized the importance of sharing that story. Boom! Fires breaking out all over the place. I'm sure by the time I write my next book, that story will have new chapters. You know what I mean? It's not our job to filter out applicants for the Kingdom of Heaven. No. Everyone we meet should get an application; it's up to them what they do with it.

Jesus does tell us that there are people who won't get it. He explains it in several places in different ways. Sometimes, no matter what you say or do, the message just lands on wet fuel. That's where the seeds of faith we talked about in Section 2 come in.

Remember that apple seed that grows into a tree that eventually births an entire apple orchard? Here's what Jesus said about that in John Chapter 4. The disciples were worried that Jesus wasn't eating enough. He told them that he had food they didn't know about by doing the will of His Father.

I get plenty of nourishment from finishing the work my Father sent me to do. You hear people say, harvest time is coming soon, but I say wake up, it's already here. The harvest I'm talking about is adding people to the Kingdom. They're paying good money for people to bring in the harvest. It's happening so fast, those who harvest the crop are catching up with those who plant the seeds!

You've probably heard people say "One worker plants seeds and another one harvests the crop" I'm telling you it's true. I sent you to collect a harvest of seeds you did not plant. Someone else planted those seeds and now you are getting the benefit.

We're also told that sometimes it's just our job to plant. That our message needs to sit with some until it catches on. Others will have a chance to see the harvest, like that woman and her friends who came to see me after I shared my story about helping her brother.

I have this conversation with people all the time. "I'm an evangelist, are you?" They smile, and say "No, of course not." I say, "I bet you are, for something."

We can't help it. If you're not evangelizing for the Kingdom, what are you evangelizing for in your life? It's something, I guarantee it. Here's what I mean.

Whether we call it being a fan, or having a hobby, belonging to a political party, or owning our own business in network marketing, we all tell people about something. Why? Because it has changed, or added something to our lives. There are Avengers evangelists and football evangelists. There are evangelists for weight loss products, brands of trucks, and cleaning products.

Whatever you're excited about, you'll find ways to work it into the conversation because it has impacted you. If Jesus is not on that list, you've got some thinking to do.

Even though I spend my days being an evangelist of the gospel of Jesus, that doesn't make me immune to becoming an evangelist for things I love. Over the years, I've been an evangelist for the Raiders, every band I've ever been in, motorcycles, albums, and movies I've loved, but a recent experience says it best.

Last year at Christmas time, the Atwood's store near my house had a sale on my favorite gun of all time—the gorgeous Springfield XD 45. When I say sale I'm not even doing it justice. It wasn't like it was just a good price. It was a phenomenal price. But it didn't end there! If you bought this beautiful handgun, it came with goodies. What kind of goodies? I'm glad you asked, because I sure did. The salesman just kept laying more stuff on the counter. The pistol of course, but that's not all. Five extra magazines. But that's not all. A case of shells. And oh, speaking of cases, here's the case for the gun too! All for a very low, low price. Quantities limited. Buy now!

Take my money! I couldn't buy it fast enough! I started going down my Christmas list to see who else deserved such a wonderful gift. In fact, before I even left the store, I messaged my best friend and even shared it on Facebook! Not only did Atwood's make a sale that day, but Springfield gained a hardcore, dyed-in-the wool evangelist. I was sharing it with everybody!

It's probably a good thing I didn't have a huge wad of cash, I'd have been like Oprah. You get a gun, and you get a gun, and you get a gun!

My wife: "Jaxx is a little young for that, Kelly!"

Seriously though, you get my point, we all talk about what excites us most. We share our favorite shows, movies, music. If we go out to eat, we share pictures and leave a Yelp review before they even bring us the check!

We are evangelism crazy in this culture. They even call people like me "brand evangelists" when we share stuff the way I did that gun. And it works!

But when it comes to the life-changing sacrifice of Jesus. Crickets.

If that's you, I'm not trying to tell you you're not saved, but you might want to check your connection. You need to renew that stuff. It goes out of date if you don't re-up once in a while. I understand though, because I was there for much of my young life. Then I checked out completely and ran as far from God as I could get. Or so I thought. Turns out David knew what he was talking about in Psalm 139

> *Is there anywhere I can go to ditch your spirit*
> *Where can I run to that I don't have to feel you?*
> *If I rocket out into space, you're there.*
> *If I bury myself alive, you're there.*
> *If I take a red eye into the rising sun*
> *To rent a hut on the most remote island*
> *Even there, I'll see your hand has guided me*
> *I'm always in the palm of your hand*
> *I can fool myself into thinking the darkness will hide me*
> *If I run into the night, it will swallow me*
> *You laugh at me, the inventor of light is not fooled by darkness*
> *To you the night and day are as one*

The same God who'd claimed me as a boy just wouldn't give up. He followed me, keeping me alive until I was ready. When it finally happened, I wasn't quite ready to let go of my world. He was okay with that. As my transformation from the Rock-and-Roll life, to developing a Kingdom mindset took place, God was patient.

After a few months of conversations back and forth with God, one day He challenged me.

—— *Chapter Seventeen* ——

SHARE IT, I DARE YOU

I'd been reading something from the Bible that really stuck with me. As I went about my day, I heard God say, "Share that thought."

"What?"

"On Facebook. It's important."

"What? No. Not gonna happen."

"What are you afraid of?"

"Everything. Maybe you're immune to ridicule and losing all your friends, but I'm not. No thanks. They already think I'm a freak. I'm in this, but let's just leave them out of it."

"Share it."

"No."

"I dare you."

I had built up this dark twisted fantasy of how people were going to react and I just knew it was going to be a bloodbath. But I finally came to a point where I realized that if I was really going through with this following-Jesus thing, sooner or later it would come down to this. It's a required part of joining the team.

Jesus has a lot to say about it and one of those places is in Matthew Chapter 10. He's finished the "basic training" part of discipleship 101 and He's about to send the disciples out to do ministry on their own for the very first time. He stands up to give them a pep talk.

Okay, guys, this is it, the big day. I know you're excited but I want to take a minute to tell you what to expect. There's no other way to say this, but I'm sending you out there like defenseless sheep into a pack of hungry wolves. All right, all right, I know this isn't what you wanted to hear, but I need you to remember, you have to remain blameless. I need you to be innocent like a dove. But, on the other hand, be shrewd like a snake. Stay on your guard!

I can see the disciples losing their enthusiasm as he goes through the list of things they'll suffer: beatings, arrests, being cursed. It sounds like so much fun, right? But to their credit, not one of them checked out. They were in it. They had a real connection to Jesus' message already and it made them ready to suffer. That's what I'm talking about, that attitude right there.

As he gets down to the end of his message, he switches gears a bit. He's warned them, now he wants to encourage them.

Don't worry about it, I'll share their secrets with you. Nothing that's hidden will stay that way. And here's what I want you to do. Those secrets that I whisper to you, I want you to shout them from the top of a house so everyone can hear you. But, don't be afraid of them. Seriously, they can only kill your body, not your soul. The only one you should fear is the one that can destroy both your body and soul.

SHARE IT, I DARE YOU

Then Jesus says something I don't really think converts well into modern English and it feels more than a little random. Almost like He's realized He's been too heavy and wants to end on a lighter note.

Look, you know how cheap sparrows are. What's the going rate? Like two for a penny? Here's the thing, as much of a disposable thing as sparrows are to you, they're not to God. He tracks every one. Even if one of them falls out of the sky, He sees and cares. He's numbered each hair on your head. He knows you and he values you more than thousands of sparrows.

When I read this, I have to remind myself this is the God of the universe talking and not the world's worst motivational speaker, but then He brings it all home. Again, I think that's just because it doesn't translate well into English and the modern world. I'm sure the disciples were nodding along.

So, when you're out there, don't be afraid to talk about me. I mean it. It's okay. I'll make you a deal, if you claim me and teach others to follow what I've taught you, I'll make sure God knows your name. I'll personally vouch for you with my father. But, if you can't do that, it will be evidence that we never really had a connection and I can't vouch for strangers.

So, here I am, knowing this, and having a choice to make. Sure, He might give me another chance. Then again, I could die without getting it. I knew what had to be done. I pulled out my phone and typed the post.

"There, is that good enough?"

"Uh, I think you meant 'you're' not 'your' but otherwise it's fine."

I told you my version of Jesus is a bit sarcastic.

So, I hit the post button and cringed, waiting for my social world to implode on top of me. But, that's not what happened. What happened was kind of anticlimactic. Nothing much. A few people liked it. I got a couple of comments, but no sarcastic rants, no obscenities.

It was weird. It was like God had my back and people weren't quite as opposed to talking about Him as I'd imagined. I'd pictured the Jell-O hitting the fan. I would lose credibility and friends, but none of that happened.

After that, God continued to prompt me about what to share and I kept obeying. Amazingly, I didn't get the backlash I expected. For the longest time, I kept waiting for it to happen. I did see a few friends who were hardcore atheists, unfriend me, but overall the response was positive and not nearly as dramatic as I'd imagined. I mean, you read those Biblical warnings, you kind of expect to experience some pain.

But that's not the end of the story. While the response wasn't much to write home about, a few months into my experiment, I got a message. I didn't even see it at first, because it was in that secret message box. You know. It's the one Facebook reserves for the disconnected souls not on our friend's lists that dare to defy the social order and private message us as strangers. When I finally opened it, I was stunned.

"Thanks for being obedient to God and sharing the messages you've been putting out over the last few months. I know you don't know me, but I've been following you and this has meant so much to me. I know it was a struggle for you, but I'm here to tell you, God told you to do this for me. God has inspired so much change in my life through your posts."

People were watching me. Me? I was barely a few months into this new chapter of my life, and not only were people watching me, but I was encouraging them. It didn't seem possible, but there it was on Facebook messenger, so it had to be true. That got me thinking about who else was watching.

I didn't make the connection quite yet. Back to my early firebug days—I was on fire, and people were showing up just to watch me burn. You have them too. Trust me. As soon as you declare, even quietly, that you are a follower of Jesus, at the first whiff of smoke from your fire people will pay attention. Why? They want to see what it's all about.

They've experienced plenty of phonies. They want to know if Jesus' message is too good to be true, or if maybe some of his followers are legit. They are fruit inspectors. They want to see if what you say lines up with how you live and the impact your life has on others.

Chapter Eighteen

SECONDHAND JESUS

When you get on fire for Jesus, make no mistake, the "firefighters" will come too. They'll do their best to try to put you out. Some of them simply don't believe anyone should ever believe in God and they want to put you out with science or philosophy, and prove your beliefs aren't practical. They will fight to discredit anything you say about God, especially if you give God actual credit for any good in your life. Don't take it personally.

They're fighting their own battles. They have no peace, so when they see you living in peace and offering it to others, they'll call you a fraud. Their lack of peace robs them of joy, so they'll poke holes in all your trial balloons at positive messaging about Jesus. They simply cannot believe that there is joy anywhere to be found in this world. That's their choice. But the thing that will make them hate you more than anything else, is if you are bold enough to unconditionally love all of your fellow humans. This will enrage them beyond belief.

Ironically, although they claim there is no moral law giver, they will be the most dogmatic defenders of a morality that excludes many from even having status in the human race. They simply cannot calculate how you can love those you whole heartedly disagree with. Any love they do experience is conditional. It's based on their behavior, or belief in one thing or another, or belonging to this or that school of thought. They'll pretend to throw logic and reason at you.

Listen, I get it. I do. A lot of Christians are out there sharing things that just don't make sense. They spout off and use scripture in ways it was never intended to be used. They claim the moral high ground on issues they simply don't understand and even argue against clearly observable facts. These firefighters lump us all into one category and if they've met one "Jesus freak" who does this or that or the other, then you must believe it too.

How do we handle this? Simple. Often we just don't respond. We just love them actively, through serving them in whatever way they need. Sometimes we have to go through some things we'd rather not. It's part of the job. Since God says He doesn't want anyone to perish, that means we have to treat them all as salvageable. All of them. No, even those people. We don't get to choose.

Sometimes we get this idea that Jesus did choose. After all, He was violently opposed to the Pharisees. Well, yes and no. He opposed their abuse of power. He opposed their willingness to let people suffer without helping them. But he loved them. He spent quite a bit of time with a few of them, even struck up a friendship with Nicodemus.

In fact, every time we think we know who can be excluded from an invite to the Kingdom, Jesus tells us we're wrong. The poor, the sick, the lonely, the broken, the sinners, the whores, and the tax collectors were all welcome. His dealings with the Pharisees were more like a father who finds out his children are lording it over each other and He wants to put a stop to it. He doesn't try to convert them. Instead, He points them back to their own scripture and asks them to reexamine their own behaviors.

It's like the antismoking campaigns of the nineties. If you're old enough to remember, for a while there, secondhand smoke was the central enemy of American media. It was on TV, every radio ad break mentioned it. It was in the magazines, plastered across our billboards and bus-stop benches.

I remember as a kid being terrified about it. On one occasion I was going into a restaurant with my parents when a woman turned and blew smoke in my face. My eyes grew wide, my throat constricted, and my pulse raced. I was terrified. I rushed away from her as fast as I could and experienced my first panic attack.

"What's wrong with you, Kelly?" my mother asked.

I was crying by this point.

"Secondhand smoke! That lady blew smoke in my face. I'm going to get cancer, Mom. I'm going to die! I'm too young to die. It's not fair. Why did she do that?"

I'm guessing my mom had to choke back hysterical laughter to deal with me at that point. I'd taken that marketing message so much to heart that it had triggered a primal response in me. My body couldn't defend itself from the signals of fear and panic my brain was pumping out.

I think this is a lot like the version of God the Pharisees had, and the version of Jesus a lot of those firefighter types are reacting to. I was terrified of secondhand smoke, but what I should be worried about is secondhand Jesus. It's killing off the fire in a lot of believers, and keeping a lot more people from ever getting lit. Secondhand Jesus is all about the rules. Secondhand Jesus is about being a "good person," and "personal holiness," and "doing the right thing," just for the sake of claiming to do the right thing. It's all about posturing and appearing righteous.

People with secondhand Jesus go to church every time the doors are open, whether that's the best place for them to be or not. They're not connected to the living God of the Bible in any way, except that they use a lot of the same language and claim to understand every word of the Bible.

In fact, secondhand Jesus is exactly what Jesus talks about in Matthew 7 when He tells us about some folks that look and sound like believers. You'd probably think they were legitimately on fire for God if you didn't know better. It's easy to mistake them for the real deal.

Not everybody who claims to be my friend gets to do Kingdom with us. There are a lot of people who will show up, claiming they know me, they'll call me Lord in front of their friends, they'll even brag about people they've prayed for to be healed, and demons they've cast out. But, in their hearts, it's not real. It's going to break my heart to look them in the eye and say, "I never knew you" but there's no real connection there. I have to send them away.

But, before you start making a list of people who are in that category, be careful. Jesus didn't start out this passage condemning anybody. In fact, it was just the opposite, He tells us a kind of funny parable about two guys, and one of them is us.

Listen, don't judge, are you paying attention? Here's how this works, however you judge others, that's how you'll be judged. If you use a heavy standard to condemn your brothers and sisters, they'll return the favor, and so will I. Whatever grace or judgement you deal out, it's coming back to you.

Look, it's silly anyway.

At this point, I picture him picking up a branch, and a little chip of bark as props.

It's kind of like this. You see your friend walking around, and he's got this chip of bark in his eye. This chip of bark represents something you think of as sin. When you see it, you immediately think to yourself, wow, I can't believe he'd do that. But it doesn't stop there. You start harassing him about how he lives his life and how much he needs to change to please God.

He chooses Peter and He has him hold this chip of bark over his eye as He continues his lesson, pointing to Peter.

Meanwhile, you're walking around with this giant branch sticking out of your eye, everywhere you go, people are having to duck to avoid this problem in your life, but you can't see it.

Meanwhile, Jesus is swinging this branch with it sticking out from his eye, as he turns this way and that, and disciples are ducking out of the way. I picture it this way because guys are guys, and if you put thirteen guys on the road together, there is going to be jokes. All the way back to the beginning of time, there would be jokes. It's just how we are.

So, what can you do about this situation? It's pretty amazing that you can even see that tiny speck in your friend's eye, when you have this giant branch sticking out of your own, isn't it? That's what you look like when you start telling people how to live their life, when they haven't even asked. First, you might want to find a gardener to help you take the branch out of your eye. Then, you can truly come to your friend and help them with their speck.

With Jesus, it's always like this. He puts the burden on us first. He assumes we've done everything we can to help the guy who's claiming Jesus but looks and sounds nothing like Him. He wants us to be compassionate first and compassionate after. There is no room with Him for celebrating someone's failure. That's not how the Kingdom is supposed to work. We are our brother's keepers.

Chapter Nineteen

NO EFFECTIVE WAY TO MAKE THAT HAPPEN

We are called to love God, love others, and be the servant of all. If you're ever tempted to believe this isn't true, just look to Paul's description of Jesus' attitude in Philippians Chapter 2. This is one of the most inspiring verses in the whole Bible to me, and it completely illustrates what a life on fire for God should look like.

Listen, if Jesus, being God, didn't think he should walk in and remind us, hey, I'm God, maybe we should imitate his attitude. Instead of lording it over anyone, he showed up, rolled up his sleeves and got to work serving. Not just serving, but serving like someone who is working off a debt.

He wasn't just humble to make a point. He was being obedient in a humble way. He was humble all the way to the cross and even as his own creation took his mortal life. This is why God made his name famous above every other name, in all of history. So that when people hear the name of Jesus everyone will bow their knees in acknowledgement of His position.

It's hard for the people who come to put you out, to fight an attitude like that. In order to do that, they need to remove one or more of the angles of the Fire Triangle. They've got to cool your heat, remove your fuel, or suck up all the oxygen. If following Jesus is just a hobby, or it's done out of fear, it's possible they can put you out.

If you're one of those who brags a lot about knowing Jesus, but there's no fire, and the only evidence in your life is like secondhand smoke, they'll have little trouble smothering your spark. If your knowledge and experience of serving God is shallow, done for show, kicking your fuel aside is not much of a challenge. And if they can discredit you, they will rob you of your oxygen, because no one wants to follow someone who's proven to be a fraud.

So, how do you become unstoppable? How do you get to the point that your fire can't be put out? I thought about this for a long time. I struggled with it, because I wanted that for my life. I could see that the apostles had it. I could see that other believers down through the centuries had reached that stage. No matter what tragedy came their way, nothing could snuff out their faith. I even knew a few Christians personally, who I thought could fit that category. What made them different?

The more I thought about it, the more apparent it became. These people were hugely influential. Not just some of the time, but everywhere they went, and with everyone they talked to. Even people who thought Christianity was bunk acknowledged the truth of who they were, honored their integrity, and complimented their service to others. They even made their enemies to come to peace with them. How?

So, I looked at the firefighters for an answer and thought through the tactics they could use. Once a person is truly convinced of the truth of the gospel, there's no way to separate them from God, so removing the heat was out. Since fuel comes from internal as well as external sources, there wasn't a way for them to cut that off, but your oxygen was still an option. Or was it.

Once again, I came back to my original revelation and heard God's voice echo, "Google It" so I went back to the Fire Triangle Article on Wikipedia. This is what I found.

In large fires where firefighters are called in, decreasing the amount of oxygen is not usually an option because there is no effective way to make that happen in an extended area.

Then I realized, it was all about scale. As long as you remain a contained camp fire, suppression is possible. You can be discredited; you can be isolated from your community and audience. But once you go full wildfire, there is no effective means of fighting it. You're going to continue to burn until all available fuel or oxygen is used up, or you burn out.

This is why, even when they fall from grace, many Christians get back up, repair the damage and go right back to spreading the Word. The coals of that fire burn forever. They never go out. Once God gets ahold of a soul like that, their impact long outlives their own mortal lives. There's a somewhat humorous story that illustrates my point in 2 Kings Chapter 13.

It starts with Elisha, Elijah's number one apprentice. You remember Elijah, the guy that called down fire from heaven and beheaded 450 prophets of Baal in front of the king and all of the nation of Israel. He was a bad dude, I mean one time he got called bald by some kids, and he called a bear out of the woods to eat them. He was so in touch with God that he's only one of two men in the Bible to never die. Enoch was one, Elijah was the other. He was taken up into heaven in a whirlwind of fire. Whoa! Talk about getting lit!

So, the day this was supposed to happen, Elijah kept trying to ditch him. It turns out to be a test with a big reward. (Another lesson about obeying God that I just love.)

I need you to stay here, Elisha, God is sending me to Bethel.

But Elisha refuses to fall for it.

Not gonna happen, as long as God is alive, and you are alive, I'm not going anywhere.

They go to Bethel where some of Elijah's students were; they came out to talk to Elisha.

So, you know your boss is getting scooped up into heaven today, right?

Elisha's reply is kind of cryptic.

Yeah, but I don't want to talk about it.

Then Elijah tries to ditch him for a second time.

Listen, Elisha, seriously, stay here. God is sending me over to Jericho.

Elisha's answer is the same as before.

Ain't gonna happen.

So, they go to Jericho to see some more prophets. They come out and talk to Elisha again.

So, you know God's taking your boss today, right?

Yep, don't wanna talk about it.

Elijah tries one last time.

Elisha, please, stay here. God is sending me over to the Jordan.

If I told you once, I've told you three times, man. You're not getting rid of me that easily.

So, they go on down to the river Jordan. Whether Elijah just hated getting his feet wet, or for old time's sake he decides one more miracle is in order. As fifty prophets come down to the river to watch, he rolls up his cloak and smacks the water. The whole river parts down the middle and Elijah and Elisha walk across on dry land.

Finally, it seems the test is about to be over. Elijah stops, looks at his friend, and says.

I'm about to leave.

I know.

So, before I go, let me grant one request for you. What will it be?

With Elijah's resume, Elisha could have asked for riches, or fame, or whatever he desired. He's not quite Aladdin's Genie, but he's got a pretty solid connection with God. Elisha, for his part, wasn't there for the prizes. He asked for one simple thing.

I want a double portion of your spirit.

The Bible doesn't tell us exactly what that means, but when you look at Elisha's ministry after this moment, it becomes clear. He's asking for twice the ability to speak and work miracles for God that his boss had. That's a tall order and Elijah tells him so.

You're asking for a lot, but you'll get it under one condition. If you see me taken into heaven, it will be yours.

Then as they're walking along, one of the very coolest pictures of God as fire takes place right before Elisha's eyes. A fiery chariot and horses swoop down out of heaven, right between them. It scoops up Elijah and carries him up into heaven like a whirlwind. I know I said some stuff about tornadoes and weather, and how Okies are used to them. But I have to admit, I've never seen a tornado of fire—although I think it would be awesome, and terrifying.

Elisha shouts:

Father, my father, the chariots and horsemen of Israel!

In a moment so perfect no screenwriter could do better, Elijah's cloak that had been witness to everything, floats down out of the sky. Elisha is so overcome with emotion he can hardly stand it. He tears his own clothes in two, picks up the cloak, walks back to the Jordan, and parts it! There's a new prophet in town.

—— *Chapter Twenty* ——

DESIRE TO GO FULL WILDFIRE

I wish we had enough pages to talk about everything Elisha got up to, because it's amazing and I highly recommend you read his life story starting from this passage forward to his death. For the purpose of this book, I want to skip to that moment—that moment of Elisha's death. It's kind of ironic in a way. After all the drama surrounding Elijah's departure, you'd think this dude who got a double helping of the spirit of Elijah, and worked so many incredible miracles in Israel, would rate a cool death scene. But here's what the Bible says in 2 Kings 13:20

Elisha died and was buried.

Wait. What? No description, no weeping prophets, no flaming chariot? Just kicked the bucket and thrown into a hole? That's it? But is it?

That's the thing with those of us who choose to get lit with God. It's never really the end of the story, and if you read just a few more verses you come to the part that illustrates my original point. I know, I came the long way around, but it's too good of a story to not tell!

It seems that after Elisha's death, Israel was plagued with Moabite raiders who would sweep in every spring to plunder and pillage. So, as it happened, a man died, and like they do, his friends went to bury him. While they were digging his grave, they saw horses in the distance and since it was Moabite raiding season, they figured they'd better hurry. So, here's what they did.

They threw this man's cold dead body into another grave. What they didn't know was whose grave it was. So, picture it.

"Listen Shem, we need to hurry, if those Moabites catch us and steal dad's best camel again, we're dead men."

"Cool it Lemuel, we still need to bury this guy. We can't just leave him here!"

Lem looks around for a minute.

"Hey, I got an idea, what about that cave over there? Looks like a tomb already. No one will ever know!"

Shem gazes across the plains, the horses are getting closer.

"Fine, grab his ankles, let's do this!"

"Okay, on three!"

"Wait, are we throwing him on three, or like, counting to three, then throwing him?"

So, eventually, they settle on a method and toss this guy into the grave and turn to run for the camel.

"Wait! Hey! You can't just leave me here!"

Lem looks at Shem.

"Did you say that?"

"Nope!"

Both white as a sheet, they turn to see their previously-dead friend running out of the cave. It seems that as soon as his corpse touched the bones of the prophet Elisha, who was buried in that tomb, the man came right back to life. The Bible never says another word about it. Imagine that!

Now that's a fire no one can ever put out.

It makes me want to do more. It drives me to share with as many people as I can, this desire to go full wildfire. That kind of crazy service is what has been driving me for quite some time. In the process of writing this book, God spoke to me. It was one of the clearest messages I've ever heard.

Although God is everywhere, I find there is something about sacred spaces that speaks to me, so I like to pray as I walk around the sanctuary of the church where I serve. It was during one of these times that I felt God speaking.

"Get ready to go."

"Okay, where am I going?"

"When they call, say yes."

That was it. There are times when God says a lot, so much you have to go over and over it to get it all. But sometimes it's just bullet points. Get ready. Say yes. It can make you wonder if you really heard Him. Sometimes, those messages never really line up with a specific circumstance, but I think that's on me. Other times, like this time, I understood it as clear as day.

If you've never heard God's voice, or you're just not sure, don't stress about it. Really. It's okay. Even some of the greatest giants of faith in human history have struggled with receiving messages from the divine. One of my favorite stories about this comes from the life of Samuel. He stands out as one of the very few men in scripture to serve God with no major moral failings that we're told of. He was faithful to the end.

Samuel was the child of Hannah, a woman who desperately wanted motherhood. So much so that she would travel to Shiloh—where the Ark of the Covenant was being kept until the building of the temple—and pour her heart out to God begging to conceive. During one such incident the priest Eli heard her praying.

She was so distraught that he assumed she was drunk. When he learned the truth, his heart was moved. He told the woman to go home and not to worry because God would answer her prayer. When Samuel was born, Hannah brought him to the priest at Shiloh to serve in worship and left them there to live. We're told that prophecies, visions, and messages from God had become rare in that time, so when the young boy, Samuel, heard a voice in the night, he assumed it was Eli calling to him.

I'm here, what can I do for you?

The old man woke from his sleep and was confused.

I didn't call you, go back to bed, boy. It must have been a dream.

Then Samuel heard the voice again, and again assumed it was Eli. He had no experience with messages from God, and didn't know anyone who did.

Eli, you called to me again, what can I do for you?

If you have kids, you already know that this time the old man was irritated. I know I would be. This kid wakes me up from sleep for no good reason? It's not going to end well if he comes back, that's all I'm saying.

I didn't call you Samuel, I'm trying to sleep! Go back to bed, and please don't bother me again!

The thing was, Samuel didn't know God yet. Although he'd been brought to Shiloh where the presence of God was believed to be, he hadn't experienced it yet. There was no fire, not even a spark in this young man. So, when God called a third time, I'm sure he tried to resist, but he'd been trained to do whatever the priest needed. So he got up and went to him a third time.

Eli, I heard you calling to me, I know I did. Is there something I can do for you?

Finally, the old man catches on. He thought back to past times when God spoke, or stories that he'd heard, and started putting the pieces together. Obviously, the kid was hearing something. It must be the voice of God.

Samuel, that's not my voice you're hearing. God is speaking. Go and lie down and if He speaks again, answer Him. Say, "I'm listening God."

So, the boy did. Sometimes when God speaks, you're so excited about what He says. Then sometimes He tells you things you don't want to know. Samuel got a good dose of the second kind. God told him about Eli and how he'd failed God in the past. He explained that judgment was coming and that He was going to judge Eli and his family.

Then Samuel got to deliver the message to Eli the next morning. Good times. Talking to God is like asking people what they think. If you want an honest response, you don't get to choose how it turns out, so be prepared.

That's why when God talks, you experience the awe and wonder of hearing from the creator, mixed with the terror of the kinds of things He sometimes needs to tell us. That's a little of how I felt as I waited to see what God was sending me to do.

Chapter Twenty-One

THE PRISONER AND THE GUARD

I waited for weeks expecting that message to come any day. Sometimes I forget that time may mean something to me, it means nothing to God.

About two months later I got a call that I was not expecting. In fact, my first inclination was to say no. I've told you that I was in the rock-and-roll life for a long time. In fact, although my bands were never more than locally popular, I did find success as big act tour manager. So when Wang Chung needed an emergency replacement for their tour manager, their manager suggested they call me. I was not expecting it.

Now, understand that when I turned my back on that life, it was over for me. I didn't want any part of it. At first, that was partly because I didn't want to risk the changes that God was making in me. It was partly out of fear of getting pulled back in. That life is attractive and even though I'd grown sick of it, I didn't know if I'd stay that way. After all, I'd been back and forth with God a lot in my life and I was committed to making it stick this time around.

But, having heard God's voice before, and knowing that this request fit the message I'd received two months earlier, I knew I needed to say yes.

Sometimes, we start to qualify what God expects from us, and in that moment, I was thinking of the benefits I could explain to sell this idea to my wife. The only one I could come up with is that the extra money from that tour would really be a huge help to our family. So, I took down the details and went home to pack.

Most of you have probably never been on a major-label, Rock-and-Roll tour. It's messy. This particular show featured multiple bands, each with their own entourage and requirements, and as the tour manager for Wang Chung, it was my job to make sure all of our needs meshed with the needs of everybody else to keep things happy. Plus, we had demands from the tour manager who was the overseer of the whole show. Those demands had to be conveyed to our bands and crews. There were a lot of moving pieces.

If you've ever seen one of those old movies about a circus traveling from town to town on a train, it's a lot like that. Only we're on buses and planes, and with a lot more alcohol, drugs, and sex. The rumors are true. That used to be my life and I wasn't looking forward to stepping back into that world. The noise, the smells, the sights, all reminded me of a time and place in my own journey I was glad to be rid of and now I was chained to this tour for four weeks. I determined to make the best of it. I got a good grip, determined to grit my teeth and hold on.

Then God spoke again. This time He reminded me of something from the Bible. If you've been around church much at all, you've definitely heard the name Paul. He wrote or dictated the majority of the documents that make up our New Testament. He was kind of a big deal. Although he didn't walk with Jesus at first, Jesus came to him in a vision to stop him from killing Christians and turn his life around. He was blind for three days and afterwards, he started preaching that Jesus was the messiah. It was a really big deal in the church in his day. They argued over whether he was legit, or just wanted to trick them all into admitting to their faith, which was illegal.

Paul was a Pharisee and a teacher of the law, so it didn't take long for him to get up to speed on the new theology, understanding Moses and the prophets like he did, and soon he was accepted as a great teacher and helped plant many of the churches mentioned in the Bible.

That being said, he was a very vocal supporter of "The Way" (the name given to the followers of Jesus), and it ended up getting him in trouble with the Roman Empire. That's what God reminded me about.

Some of Paul's most positive, upbeat letters were written while a chain connected him to a Roman soldier. He was under house arrest sometime around 60 BC for a period of two years. During that time, it's believed, he penned Ephesians, Philippians, Colossians, and his letter to Philemon.

My conversation with God went something like this.

"So, Kelly, you think you're chained to this tour? Is it a burden for you?"

"Yeah, it kind of is. I'm not looking forward to it. It cramps my style."

"Remember Paul?"

"Yeah."

"Remember how he went to prison twice?"

"Yeah."

I didn't like where this was going. I was starting to wonder if it was God, or I was dreaming and my mom was about to put a guilt trip on me, or something. I jest, of course, but all the same it felt like a trap.

"So, he was in chains when he wrote four books of the New Testament."

"Okay, fine, he had it harder than me. I'll try to look on the bright side. I'm sorry."

"That's not my point."

"It's not?"

"No."

"Okay, what is it then?"

"Do you suppose Paul was chained to that soldier, or was the soldier chained to Paul?"

And in that moment, the creator of the universe totally flipped the script on me. It took two seconds for my entire perspective to get flipped around and upside down about going on this tour. You see, it had never even occurred to me but every prison really imprisons at least two people, the prisoner, and their guard. I'd been looking at it as if I was a prisoner of this tour, as if I was chained to it and all that this entails. But what God was showing me was that if I chose, it could be just the opposite!

My eyes opened and I started to see things differently. That soldier was chained to Paul. Whatever Paul decided to spend his time on that's what this poor guy did, all day, every day. Paul wasn't chained down and I didn't have to be either. I could choose to think of myself as chained to this tour, getting drug across the country, or I could see that this tour was chained to me and take it any direction I wanted to go. The wheels started turning.

If I was going to be in charge of this experience, how would I approach it? Obviously, I had to be a part of their schedule and agenda, but as long as I colored inside the lines, the potential was inexhaustible.

I started imagining it. I would preach the greatest revival in the history of Rock and Roll tours. Before it was over, the bands would all be singing for Jesus. That's when God laughed at me.

"Sure, you could do that Kelly, if you want them to send you home from your first city."

He was right. Of course, He was right, Him being all knowing. It's like that.

"Okay, so what then?"

"Love me, love them, serve everyone."

It's easy to see how this works in the everyday world. It may cost you something, but it's not that difficult to figure out. On tour, everything is different. Every person on a music tour has a job, and every task that needs doing is assigned to one of those people. It's like that thing highly organized people say: "A place for everything and everything in its place." I just wasn't sure how much room there was for servant leadership in the role of rock band tour manager, but I'd figure it out.

—— *Chapter Twenty-Two* ——

SIMPLY SURRENDER AND FOLLOW GOD'S PLAN

From the first night, it hit me. The smells, the sights, the sounds swept over me like a wave of nostalgia. But, instead of getting misty eyed, I just felt relief. Relief that this wasn't my daily reality anymore. The liquor was flowing, the drugs were plentiful, the young beautiful women were ready and willing. It was everything that young Kelly K had dreamed of. But it wasn't my scene anymore; it all made me feel vaguely tired and to be honest, I felt pity. Pity that all of these people at the height of their game were still trying to fill the empty places in their hearts and minds with such temporary pleasure and empty pursuits.

I didn't have time to think about it for long. If I was going to be a servant leader, there was plenty to be done. I dove right in. As soon as I knew my band was taken care of, I started looking for other ways to help. Almost immediately, one thing stuck out. The dressing rooms needed cleaning.

Don't get me wrong. They hire people to handle that job and I wasn't about to take anything away from them. But their usual job, when it's not rock bands they're cleaning up after, is mopping floors, wiping down counters, taking out trash, and polishing mirrors.

This is different because they way bands live backstage is disgusting. They never throw anything away. It's as if every lesson they ever learned about cleaning up their own mess is intentionally reverse-engineered to create the biggest possible mess.

There were beer bottles, empty food wrappers, paper cups—you name it, it was there. And it was strung everywhere. Sometimes within literal inches of a trash can. But that was someone else's job. A someone they would never see. Those faceless, nameless people they might pass on their way in or out but didn't have a clue about, would deal with it. That's what they got paid to do. But, not on my tour. I cleaned up.

It was so unusual for anyone to do anything outside of their job description that guys in the bands thought it was amazing. One night I looked up and they were filming me. They wanted to share this incredibly simple thing I was doing with their followers. What I hadn't counted on when I started was this, true service, out of a pure heart, not in pursuit of anything other than loving others, is a revolutionary act. I was waging war against darkness and bringing light into a place that needed it a lot.

Before it was over, I was running errands and doing anything I could to help anyone on the tour regardless of their job, authority, or connection. I was here to be a servant to all. One night I found myself in the tour owner/production manager's office. That's where it all kind of ground to a halt, temporarily, for me. In my mind, I'd saved him a ton of time and trouble. In his position, I'd have loved me, a band manager who actually cared. But that's not what happened.

"Hey, I just wanted to check and see if there's anything I can do for you," I said.

"Why are you even in my office? Seriously!" This guy was not grateful, or even halfway happy to see me.

"You're a band manager get the blankety-blank out! As far as I'm concerned, you're the enemy! I don't want to see your face in here again spying on me. What goes on in here is none of your blankety-blank business! Am I clear? Do we understand each other?"

I was stunned. In my line of work, you don't get cussed out often. It happens, but usually you see it coming, and almost never from someone you're serving with. I had to recognize the reality of my situation and understand that this guy was acting out of his own reality. A reality where it was my job to get every penny out of his budget that I could for my band. I was there to make them happy, and more famous and successful. He was there to keep as much of the tour budget for his own company as he could. In his mind, I was a necessary evil to be tolerated, but barely. So, I left.

Serving is hard. Not everyone wants to be served, and leaving that office I had to remind myself of a few simple things. First, this wasn't my world. In three weeks I'd be off the road again, back to my way of life. I didn't need this tour, I'm a preacher. They needed me. This production manager couldn't see it, but that was the truth. They'd called me, not the other way around.

Second, it just made me determined to stick to my plan. I had their attention and all I had to do was maintain my focus and attitude and the impact would happen. I just knew it. Sometimes we get a chance to see the results of our efforts almost immediately and this was one of those times. I doubled down. I worked for the production team, I worked for the other bands, I helped the stage crew, wherever I saw a need that I could fill, I stepped up like it was my job.

By the time the tour was over the production manager had done a complete 180. When it was time to say goodbye and head to our various homes, he sought me out. This time, where I had seen a scowl and the look of a man who wanted me dead, there was a huge smile.

"I owe you an apology man," he said. "I've never seen anything like it. When I see managers going a step above, it often means they want something. Some of them even want my job. It makes me defensive. But not you. You worked harder than anyone I've ever seen on a tour and you'd be welcome anytime, man. Thanks. I've never seen anyone just step up and serve everybody like you did. Thank you."

I held out my hand, but instead, he stretched out his huge arms and wrapped them around me in a hug. Where all I'd meant to do was help lighten the load, the Holy Spirit had done more. This man was changed. I don't know the condition of his heart or where he stands with God, but I do know this—for four weeks, he got to see what it means to serve Jesus. I hope it makes a difference for him. I really do.

From random people thanking me, to band members taping me, to the production manager hugging me, the four weeks were filled with evidence of what one believer, on fire for God, in a dark place, can do. They saw me. They knew I was different and it mattered. I bet the next time they go on tour I'll get mentioned, and it will be for all the right reasons. This is what spreading it is supposed to look like.

This to me, is what Jesus meant when He told His disciples not to worry what they would say in their own defense, because the Holy Spirit would put words in their mouths. In my case, the Holy Spirit replaced a whole lot of words with a few, along with a whole lot of action. But He inspired me without a doubt. It's the difference between knowing that you are His, that you are a legit part of the kingdom, and doing things for show, which often ends poorly.

Without the Holy Spirit, I could have waded into that tour like a man on fire for sure. I could have spouted a bunch of lines about personal holiness and repentance. I could have spent four weeks pointing out chips of bark in people's eyes, while all the time growing a great big tree out of my own.

Instead, I simply surrendered and followed God's plan. It's amazing what happens when we do. When we don't, it sometime goes a little like the story in Acts Chapter 19.

My boy, Paul, was in the city of Ephesus and as a Pharisee, he was welcomed into the Synagogue to teach. Now, in the Jewish tradition one teacher presents his views, and the whole congregation sits in judgement. There's a lot of back and forth to come to consensus about what things mean. However, it's supposed to be done in respect.

After Paul had been teaching in the synagogue about the Kingdom of Heaven for three months, some of the men were being completely obstinate in their opposition to him and even talking bad about The Way behind Paul's back. So, rather than continue in an environment where nothing was being accomplished, he moved to the philosopher Tyrannus' lecture hall and taught there for two years.

While he was there, God worked a lot of really cool miracles. Paul was so in tune with the spirit that if a cloth or an apron was brought to him, he would touch it and when they took it to the sick, they would recover and evil spirits would leave them instantly!

Some of the Jews from the synagogue decided they could do what Paul did. They started going around casting out evil spirits using the name of Jesus as their authority, and it worked, until one day it didn't anymore. Picture this.

These dudes from the synagogue show up to do their thing at a house. They pray over the sick person and command the evil presence to leave. But, instead of what had been happening, the tables were turned. Although they used the name of Jesus, this particular evil spirit refused to go. In fact, things got ugly.

The Jews in attendance were the seven sons of Sceva, a Jewish Chief Priest. They used the same procedure they'd been using.

In the name of Jesus, whom Paul has been preaching about, we command you to leave this body!

They'd been used to seeing an immediate change, but instead, the demon answered them back.

I know who Jesus is, I've even heard of Paul, but I don't know any of you!

From there, things went from bad to worse as this single, demon-possessed man proceeded to kick the butts of all seven of these Jewish exorcists.

Not only that, but in the process, he stripped them bare and beat them bloody. They ran out of the house naked and bleeding. Can you imagine if that happened in your neighborhood? Word would spread pretty quickly, wouldn't it?

Did you see that video on YouTube of those naked exorcists?

No, what happened?

OMG, you've got to see this, here, watch this! See, now they run out bleeding!

Are they completely nake…? Oh, yep they are!

When the word got back to the synagogue, the entire attitude changed and they developed a newfound respect for the name of Jesus. What had happened? Here's my take.

They took secondhand Jesus to an exorcism. Straight up, I think that's exactly what happened. They had heard about Jesus, saw that His name worked miracles, so they treated it like any other tool and used it. The problem was, they didn't have the correct operating system. What do I mean by that?

Paul, after being struck blind, had been anointed and received the Holy Spirit.

While these guys seemed to be doing the stuff, they were never introduced to the One Person in the Godhead that they needed to make it work. They knew the Father; He was their father too. They'd heard about Jesus, although they obviously didn't quite get the whole message. But the Holy Spirit was completely missing from their equation, and it nearly cost them their lives.

This is the difference between getting lit, staying lit, spreading it, or being a straight up secondhand Jesus arsonist. Yes, they were burning, but their strange fire finally caught up to them. The fires they had been setting weren't built on the right heat or fuel, and the oxygen became contaminated! The same thing can happen to us.

—————— *Chapter Twenty-Three* ——————

"I'M FRIENDS WITH THE BAND"

That often-ignored Person of the Holy Spirit--the one I jokingly referred to as the Ringo Star of the trinity—is the key to this entire puzzle. Make no mistake about it. Remember this. Without the life-giving power that invented light, our ability to create, maintain, or spread light is artificial at best, and a dangerous counterfeit at worst.

Think back through what we've learned about the Holy Spirit so far. First, John paints a picture of the Holy Spirit as a Baptism of Fire. This vivid imagery was the backdrop to Jesus' own baptism at John's hand. Later, Jesus tells us it's a good thing that He's leaving so He can send the "helper" to infill us with the power to serve and build the kingdom. Finally, following His crucifixion, resurrection, and ascension, we find the disciples all gathered in the upper room on Pentecost.

From nowhere, the Holy Spirit arrives in a rushing wind and flaming tongues of fire to indwell every person in the place and giving them the ability to speak in other languages. Peter is heard preaching in languages of different people from all over the world. Because of that, three thousand people believed in Jesus on that one day.

It's somewhat ironic that arguably the most dramatic entrance of all is reserved for this final member of the trinity to be introduced. Then we argue over His existence, debate what His presence is like, and often ignore, or suppress, His work. Think about it, the Father's entrance is a quiet, but confident, "Let there be light." Jesus' entrance was completely downplayed, in a tiny town, in a forgotten stable, laid in a manger and remembered only by a few shepherds until almost two years later when the wisemen show up.

The Holy Spirit shows up and blows the door off the place, makes everyone think the disciples are drunk, then proceeds to heal the sick, raise the dead, tear down prisons, and generally wreak havoc with Empire in the ancient world, and we forget all about Him. We think we can access the power of Jesus, get God's fire, without Him.

Funny thing about God speaking. When He does, it changes everything. In fact, until this tour, there were still pieces missing in my understanding of the process. I realized it had to be about access to the fire and the role of the Holy Spirit in the fire triangle, but other than what you've read already, I didn't have a clear picture of what it all meant. That is, until we reached San Antonio on our tour.

Some nights I love nothing better than to live backstage. The music, the lights, the smell of the fog, the roar of the crowd. I'm vicariously living my childhood dream of being a world-famous rock musician and it's glorious. But, somewhere after about day three of a four week tour the wonder wears off.

You find yourself bone weary. You're awake because of a combination of adrenaline and caffeine. You're beginning to realize your aging body is borderline—too old to operate twenty-four-hours a day anymore, coupled with the thinly veiled hostility of impatience that often hangs around a busy professional stage for anyone not vitally important to making the show happen, which was me. So, you leave.

That was me the night of our show in San Antonio. It wasn't as if I was miserable. The tour turned out better than I ever expected, and I wish I could say that God told me to go out front and sit and people watch by the merch tables, but that's not what happened. At least not consciously.

I wandered out through the maze of road cases and half-tuned instruments that make up a rock show's back halls. I let myself out past the guards, checking to make certain I had my lanyard, just in case the guy on duty when I got back decided to hassle me. I had it.

In the world of tours, the lanyard containing your credentials, is your lifeline. Without it, you risk wasting valuable time convincing well-meaning people who are doing their jobs, to let you do yours. With it, you feel like the Lord of the Manor. Mine was all access.

While the show is going on, one of the most peaceful places in a rock venue is the lobby. The vendors are relaxed and chatty, the concession stands are open with no lines, and you can even get into a restroom without fighting fifty people for a stall. Plus, the thump of the music is just enough to hear the full-effect version of every song in your head, at just the right volume. It's a great place to collect your thoughts and catch your breath, except for the fangirls.

Fangirls are a special breed of human. The level of dedication it takes to memorize not only every lyric and note, but the entire contents of the liner notes, every blog post, Instagram quote, and interview video of every member of your clan's demigods is impressive. Reciting it to anyone who will stand still long enough to listen, is exhausting.

That's why when the girl approached me, I braced myself for an onslaught, but I didn't really expect what came next.

"Hi, do you work back... there?" she asked, absently, waving toward the bowels of the building.

I thought about this for a second before I answered. Technically, the answer was no. I was not on this tour as a roadie, or a stage hand. I didn't have a lot of pull in the greater "carnie like" tribe that governed the land beyond those doors. In fact, their king had recently ripped my head off for offering to even help him and I wondered briefly how he would want me to answer, but she was there, obviously with a request, and I decided to engage.

"Yes."

"Okay, because I need to get in to see Wang Chung," she said.

I almost chuckled. While I had almost no power over backstage passes, or who went where beyond the security check point, I had total control over access to one musical act in this traveling sideshow and she had just named it. She continued before I could reply.

"I'm not a stalker or anything."

Said every stalker ever. It's like a law or something. They're required to declare this.

"I'm friends with the band. I've been on their bus and hung out with them. We've smoked together, you know? I know all of them..."

And this is where she downloaded her encyclopedic knowledge of the band.

"I've been to a lot of their shows, in fact..."

She seemed legit and she obviously really wanted to see them.

She wasn't panicky or demanding, just trying to prove her point. That there was a legitimate relationship between herself and the musicians I represented. Just as I was about to make her night by granting her request, she said one sentence too many and changed the whole game.

"I really don't need you," she said, leaning to look past me. "Normally I could do this on my own and I wouldn't need your help."

And there it was. The one thing she could have said to make me change my mind, other than going mad-dog crazy, or being too stoned to speak. Out of everyone she could have asked, I was perfectly aligned to grant her request instantly. In fact, I was the only one who could. I even outranked the tour owner himself on this one issue. But if she thought she could manage on her own, more power to her. I was tired, I didn't need that kind of grief, so I went and sat down.

From where I sat, I watched her hesitantly look around for a few moments, hoping against hope that some magical gate keeper would show up, but no one came. She never gave me another glance and eventually she just faded away.

The irony was so thick when I went backstage later to talk to the band. I told them about their friend out front, still convinced that she was who she said. She'd checked all the boxes, and I was a pretty cautious screener. I described the girl and told them about the experiences she'd shared.

They played their part in a stone-faced denial. They didn't know this woman. Had never met her. Couldn't remember her at all. She had been a total stalker, it seemed.

"She's no friend of ours."

I let it soak in and thought about it for a long time after, piecing together the puzzle until it occurred to me that without any big production, God had just handed me the perfect ending to this book.

The girl, me, the band, were the perfect picture of a secondhand Jesus and a lack of access to the fire of God.

This woman was like so many people sitting in Christian churches every Sunday. They think that knowing about God is enough. They're fooling themselves.

Then I wondered, have I ever done that? Have I ever looked the Holy Spirit in the eye and said, "Dude, I don't need you. I can do this on my own." When all the while that Spirit, living inside every believer, is the only gate- keeper to the fire of God.

I know I've ignored His instructions before and I think He treats me a little like I treated that girl. He steps aside and lets us try. He waits for us to exhaust our options, waiting patiently, knowing He holds the key when we're ready to acknowledge his position and submit to His leading.

As you focus on Getting Lit, Staying Lit and Spreading It, you're going to run into counterfeits. Many of them will know all about the story of Jesus. They'll quote the right verses and pray the right prayers. They'll listen to the right music and follow the right preachers. But without this connection, this indwelling presence, they're just fans of Jesus, not actually friends.

The danger is real. In fact, Jesus told his disciples that their entire world can collapse around them and you don't want to get caught in their "house" when the foundation crumbles and their lives collapse.

If I've gone over this scripture once, I'll go over it a hundred times again. In Matthew 7, this is Jesus warning about false followers.

I need you to understand that not everyone who calls me master, teacher, or Lord, is going to enter the Kingdom. It's about more than saying the right thing. It's about doing what the Father asks us to do, about carrying out His will.

There's going to be a lot of people who show up and say, we foretold the future in your name, we chased away evil spirits in your name, you know we did. You know we spoke your name and created many miracles.

But, for those who are not connected to me there's a hard truth coming. I'll be forced to look them in the eye and send them away, because I never really knew them. They know a lot about me, but because they did those things for their own purposes, they proved they didn't know me.

Anyone who hears me teach and changes their actions to line up, is like an architect who understands foundations. They build their life so that when the storm comes, they survive without a scratch.

Anyone who hears me teach and refuses to change their actions, is like an architect who skipped foundations 101, when the storm comes, their house is built on sand and when it collapses, the damage will be severe.

Don't let this scare you though. This scripture says those who do the will of the Father WILL inherit His Kingdom. You may be saying, "that's easy for you Kelly, you know what the will of God is for your life. You're an Evangelist! But what about me?" Well, I'm glad you asked.

Remember Matthew 5? When it said, YOU are the light of the world. No one hides their light, they let it shine for all to see. So that others may see their good deeds, and give glory to the Father. Remember that? That, right there, IS the will of God for your life. Want me to simplify it even more? I think you already know what I'm going to say, don't you?

The will of God for your life, my life, and every person on Earth, is to Get Lit, Stay Lit, and Spread It!

——— *Chapter Twenty-Four* ———

THEY'LL THANK HIM FOR SENDING YOU

When I first came across the fire triangle, I was so excited about the simplicity of its message. It was a great way to take such a complex subject as knowing and serving God and put it into bite-sized chunks. The more I've dug into it through the time I've spent preaching it and writing about it, the more it starts to fit like a well-worn shoe.

That's why I wanted to wrap this book up with a quick reminder of what we're doing here. We are launching a new generation of the most exciting marketing campaign that's ever come to planet earth. We are signing up to volunteer for the biggest rescue mission in history. We're building a city on a hill that's filled with light, and joy, and love. And I can't wait to be there with all of you. In a way, we already are.

But that all depends on us as individuals and how much we take this message to heart. Because there's a hurting world out there that needs light, and we are the ones who are tasked with delivering it. As we finish this book and look to the future, I want to encourage you to not think about what you've read here and just nod your head. If you are not already completely on fire, with a life giving, nourishing flame, I want to encourage you to ask God to show you what that's like. He will.

That's the first step in becoming a living, thriving member of God's construction crew. As you step into that role, you'll find that the fuel is readily available. But only if you're willing to put it in the tank. You've got to consume God's word regularly and learn, as Paul said in Philippians Chapter 4:

I'm going to wrap this up fam, I'm talking to all of you. Whenever you see truth, find nobility, see someone doing the right thing, whenever you find purity, beauty and things that are worthy to be admired- if you ever see, hear or experience anything that should be encouraged and praised! Focus on that, think on that, bury that in your heart and meditate on it.

That my friends, if you act on it, is the essence of fuel. It's a great thought to carry through your day. Look for things that look like Jesus and celebrate them! Wherever you find them, whether in church or not.

Remember, matches and kindling don't make fire on their own. You've got to choose to act on what you read. Lay a foundation under your life and keep that fuel stocked up, so you don't end up like the five foolish chicks who missed the wedding. The Kingdom of God, much like fire, is an event, not a thing, and it is happening all around us. If our lamps run out of oil, the whole scene will happen without us. I don't know about you, but I don't want that.

I think, if anything, this second part of staying lit is probably the toughest thing to do. Remember this: even if you burn down to a coal, and you may, God's Holy Spirit will blow and ignite that fire in you again, and again, and again. That connection is forever and He never gives up on us, even when we give up on ourselves.

Lit and staying lit? Great, then you're ready my friends, and it doesn't take much to make that fire spread. A few things to remember. Once you're lit, people are watching, and some will try to snuff you out. If they do, it's because you let them.

Determine right now to watch for it, and fight that with everything you've got. The world needs real believers right now. There are plenty of strange fires perverting Jesus' teachings.

Try to remember what we learned from Paul in Philippians Chapter 2, and don't get a big head. Jesus came as a servant. If he came and worked like He was working off a debt, then what should we do but follow in His steps? This humility, this love-God, love-others, serve-everyone pattern is the only way it works. Everything else is secondhand Jesus and you know where that ends up.

Finally, beware of burnout. It happens to the best of us. Even Elijah. When you start to feel like you're the only one, look me up, call a friend, lean on family (if they are believers), check in with a pastor, but know that you are not alone. Not by a long shot. God's got a kingdom full of people who've got your back. We've been through it. Nothing you do, or say, or experience, is going to separate you from His love, and we're here to help you get back on track.

I'm excited for you. My part in this mission is over with most of you. I've let my light shine and hopefully you've caught the spark. And always remember, THIS is your job. Your commission. Your challenge. Now go out into the world, whatever that looks like for you, and Get Lit, Stay Lit, and Spread It! So, on that note, I'll leave you with the words of Jesus from Matthew 5.

Just as I am the light, you are the light of this dark world. If you build a town on a hill, it would be hard to hide it from travelers, wouldn't it? You are that town, that city, that Kingdom, and it's like your own lamps at home. When you light them, you don't put bowls over them, do you? That would be crazy. That's what lampstands are for, like that city on a hill, they lift the lamp up, where the light can spread into every corner of your home so that everyone can see better.

Listen carefully, this is what I want for you. I want you to be like that city, like that lampstand. I want you to burn so bright in front of people that they can see the good things you're doing. When they do, they'll know you belong to God and they'll thank Him for sending you.

ABOUT THE AUTHOR

Kelly K is a Husband, Father of four, Preacher, Teacher, Writer and Motivational Speaker. Preaching the love of Jesus in a manner that is both progressive and passionate. Kelly K is a highly sought-after conference speaker, and social media E-vangelism teacher. His messages reach out to inspire and encourage millions of lives through many multimedia platforms.

Kelly K's approach to speaking focuses on bridging the gap of cultures, ages, and society by offering a sound that is relative to every listener. His message is one of love, faith, joy and hope in Jesus Christ. Kelly K travels to any distance to share this amazing reckless love of Jesus and offer a new perspective on how reach a world that is used to tuning out anything even slightly "religious". So many have been blessed by the words, love and passion of Kelly K.

Kelly K currently lives in Kingfisher, Oklahoma with his beautiful wife Lindsay, and his four children, Brennen, Chase, Avery, and Jaxx. He is the staff Evangelist for LifeWay Church of Kingfisher.

Also from Kelly K

KELLY K

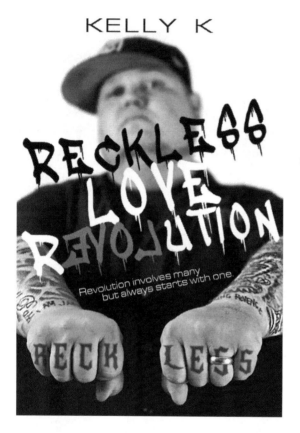

Available on Amazon!

or by going to:

www.KellyKMinistries.com

It's easy to hate, it takes true character to love those who will never love you back. In Reckless Love Revolution, we will explore the way Jesus loved people recklessly. How to give without expecting anything in return. Love others the way they would want to be loved. Understand that people are not projects. Always assume the best in people. Love the lonely, feed the hungry, and bandage the broken. (Remember when that was you?) When you love others, lives will change. Starting with yours. Reach out to people, never reach down. Love as if your life depends on it. Love recklessly, Love extravagantly, Love loud. A revolution involves many, but it always starts with one.

Connect with Me

Follow Kelly K on social media for daily posts, videos, sermons, Bible studies, and more!

- facebook.com/TheKellyK
- @KellyK_13
- YouTube.com/KellyKMinistry

www.KellyKMinistries.com

To request Kelly K to come speak at your church or event, please email:

KellyKopp@Gmail.com

To give into this ministry:

PayPal.me/KellyKMinistry

Made in the USA
Middletown, DE
25 October 2023

41387761R00099